Snakes & SCORPIONS

MEMOIRS

Cirencester

Published by Memoirs

MEMOIRS
PUBLISHING

25 Market Place, Cirencester, Gloucestershire, GL7 2NX
info@memoirsbooks.co.uk www.memoirspublishing.com

Printed in England

CHARACTERS

❦

Taniya and Maaria	- sisters and daughters-in-law
Ajmal	- father-in-law
Nagina	- mother-in-law
Fardeen	- Taniya's husband, the son of Ajmal and Nagina
Feroz	- Maaria's husband, also the son of Ajmal and Nagina
Aaliya	- Ajmal's daughter, sister of Fardeen and Feroz
Jamil and Haroon	- sons of Ajmal and Nagina
Nargus	- Nagina's mother and Ajmal's mother-in-law
Kiran	- Nargus' daughter and Nagina's younger sister
Moeen	- Nargus' youngest son, Nagina and Kiran's brother
Shahid	- Ajmal's younger brother
Sobia	- Shahid's wife
Shiza	- Ajmal's sister
Sheroz	- Ajmal's cousin

INTRODUCTION

Snakes and scorpions is the story of two young, innocent sisters who did not know how cruel some people could be until it was too late. They had no idea what nightmare they were going to face by marrying two brothers with evil, selfish parents. All their husbands wanted to do was marry the sisters to stay in the UK and abuse them. The marriages ended after the women were beaten up by their husbands. This story is told the way it happened to explain the torture and suffering both sisters had to go through.

This book is dedicated to my son Adam, whom I love so much. He should know the truth about his father and his family.

CHAPTER ONE

Ajmal Rafiq has said to both his sons: 'It does not matter how you earn money even if you break the law or commit fraud, as long as the money goes to Pakistan'.

Ajmal does not care about anyone but himself. He does not care about his sons or his own family. He has hardly given anything to his sons, and when he does give something he takes it back from them again. He has been taking money from people all his life. He owes many innocent people money.

Ajmal Rafiq owes our family £4000, plus £2000 which he borrowed from my family before his son Fardeen's wedding in 1997. He also owes my family money for air tickets to and from Pakistan.

In 1997 Ajmal Rafiq committed fraud on more than 10 banks in the UK. He had two houses on mortgages. He ran off to Pakistan with the mortgage money of £100,000 and built a house in Mirpur. The first house he built kept collapsing, and the latest one is now falling apart too.

All the electronic goods Ajmal took to Pakistan and put in his house were stolen. He bought them on credit cards and did not pay the bill.

Ajmal thought his son Fardeen could stay in the UK, and he had a chance to split him up from his wife. That was why he started the fight in the first place, for revenge, to get back at Fardeen's father-in-law for not doing his son's marriage with his daughter.

Ajmal Rafiq's mother-in-law Nargus is also responsible for splitting Ajmal's son Feroz up with his wife. She has brainwashed Feroz, telling him lies and turning him against her. She has also turned him against his father and his grandfather Raja Azhar and his family.

Nargus swears at Ajmal and his father and family in front of Feroz. Nargus has turned her daughter Kiran against her husband. She is also responsible for their fights. Kiran swears at her husband and makes him do all the housework after he comes back from work. She also talks behind people's backs and causes fights between couples. When her daughter Kiran's husband hit Kiran, her son Moeen beat him up and they called the police. Then Nargus and Kiran threw him out of their house. He had to spend several months in a rented flat.

Nargus swears at her sons-in-law all the time. She and her granddaughter would say about Kiran's husband, 'If we beat him and throw his body somewhere no one will know because he has no relatives in England to run to'.

Ajmal's daughters-in-law Taniya and Maaria have seen how Kiran treats her own husband. When he comes home from work she feeds him, and then when he is about to sit down to rest she tells him to wash all the dishes. It takes him an hour to wash all the dishes, and then he has to mop the floor and put the rubbish out. He rolls his sleeves down and goes to sit down, but then Kiran tells him it's his turn to make the tea. She sits down and laughs at him. She has no shame about the way she treats him. She should sort out her own marriage before interfering with other people's.

Nargus' daughter-in-law Neelam is responsible for turning her husband Moeen against his older brother. She is also responsible for splitting up Feroz Rafiq from his wife by phoning him, telling him how much she misses him and making him go to Accrington all the time.

In 1993 Ajmal's daughter-in-law's family thought Ajmal and his family were going back to Pakistan, so Ajmal's daughter-in-law's mother gave Ajmal's wife and daughter suits. She also gave Ajmal's daughter gold bangles as a gift. Next we hear she is telling everyone she is engaged. A few months later the family heard that Ajmal's daughter, who was only 12 years old, was going around telling everyone that she was engaged to her sister-in-law's brother. Ajmal Rafiq's daughter-in-laws' family did not even know this and were very shocked.

When Ajmal's daughter was 13 years old she said to her sister-in-law's mother 'Remember, when I get married, I want to be laden with gold from head to toe.' No one had even asked for her *rishta* (hand in marriage).

When Ajmal Rafiq and his wife Nagina, Nargus' daughter, were in England, they were too busy making money to care about their children. In 1997, when Ajmal and Nagina were about to go back to Pakistan, Nagina cried in front of her daughter-in-law's parents and said to them that she did not feel as though she had a daughter any more. Nagina said her mother had turned her daughter against her and would not give her daughter back to her. When she asks her mother for her daughter back she says that if she tries to get her back she will call Social Services.

She also said her mother was taking her daughter to the homes of her enemies.

Nagina said she did not recognise her own daughter when she passed her in the street. She said her mother had changed her daughter completely and Nagina asked how she could give her daughter's *rishta*.

Nagina Ajmal said she couldn't even talk about anything in her own house because her daughter would go running to tell her mother everything.

Nagina also said her mother Nargus was making her daughter dance at other people's weddings, the weddings of people they do not talk to. When they walk along the street those same people laugh at Nagina and Ajmal because they know they do not talk to them, yet their daughter dances at their weddings.

Everything was then sorted out in Birmingham and Ajmal and his wife went back home to Accrington.

In 1997 Ajmal Rafiq cried in front of his daughter-in-law's father, begging him to give his daughter's hand in marriage to his son Fardeen. Ajmal's daughter-in-law's father replied, 'How can I give my daughter's hand in marriage to your sons, because none of your families are happy?' And Ajmal had said, 'As long as I'm alive no one will look at your daughters horribly'.

Ajmal begged again and said, 'Please give your small daughter's *rishta* to my son Fardeen. If you do you'll do me a big favour, and I'll always be grateful to you. If you don't I will be ruined because I have no money and if my son Fardeen gets his stay it will be a big help to me.' But his daughter-in-law's father wasn't sure Ajmal would keep his word.

When Ajmal's daughter-in-law's father called his father Raja Azhar to tell him the good news about the marriage proposal, he said 'If you give your daughter's hand in marriage to Ajmal's son I won't take any responsibility because Ajmal took a loan out with the bank. He told them they could have my house and I would have been on the streets because of him. Ajmal cannot be trusted'.

When Ajmal's mother-in-law Nargus found out, she quickly

phoned Ajmal's daughter-in-law's father and told him not to get his daughter married to Ajmal's son because her daughter Nagina and her husband both stole her pension book and took all her money when she was living in Pakistan at the time. He was shocked to hear this.

Ajmal's daughter-in-law's father then confronted Ajmal and asked him what was going on. Azhar and his mother-in-law Nargus had said this about him. Ajmal quickly told him not to listen to them as no one was happy about his son's marriage. That was why they were saying this, to ruin everything for him. 'They don't want my sons to settle down and have a nice life' he said.

Ajmal's daughter-in-law's father wasn't sure who to believe any more. He couldn't trust Ajmal either. On Fardeen's wedding day neither Nargus nor her daughter Kiran attended the wedding. Ajmal's daughter Aaliya was forced to come to her brother's wedding, though she didn't want to because of her Nan.

After the wedding, Nagina told Fardeen's wife that all the wedding clothes she had bought for her were bought second-hand from a woman whose daughter had run away on her wedding day and did not marry. Her mother sold it cheap to her. She looked at Fardeen's wife Taniya and said, 'What did you think you were worth anyway?'

Later Taniya found out that even the wedding suit Fardeen had worn was bought on a credit card and not paid for. She was shocked.

Ajmal had also borrowed £2000 from Fardeen's father-in-law, saying he had no money to pay for his son's wedding in Accrington. Ajmal took the money, but did not use it for his son's wedding. Instead he made an excuse that his brother-in-law Moeen was ill in hospital and he was there with him all the time. Really he had used the money for his own purposes.

In 1997, when Ajmal's daughters-in-law's family heard Nargus's son Moeen was ill with kidney failure, they felt sorry for him and prayed for him to get well. All that time Nargus was doing *taveez* (an amulet which can be used either to cure people or bring them problems. Nargus was using it to cause problems for Ajmal's daughter-in-law's brother) on their son. Her son got ill because he was drinking so much alcohol. Isn't Nargus ashamed of that?

In Pakistan Ajmal and his wife worry about honour, but what happens to their sense of honour when they come to England?

Nargus and her family all sit together and bad-mouth Ajmal's daughters-in-law all day and say they are bad Muslims. But how can they say this? All they did was listen to their parents and get married. These days most children don't listen to their parents. They play around and get married to their own choice of partner. People don't talk about them. But people do talk about the ones that listen to their parents and get married. What has the world come to?

Neelam's father begged his daughter not to marry out of the family, but she did not listen – she turned against him. Nargus was happy with that. Neelam's father cried at her wedding and told all the men in the hall that it was her fault that he had to let her marry outside the family and the caste because she had left him with no choice and had not listened to him. She answered him back, and she still does not get along with him.

He said he only gave her *rishta* to Nargus's son because they knew Raja Azhar, Ajmal's father, otherwise who would have given Nargus's son *rishtay* in the first place? Not him.

Neelam was going out with her husband four years before she was engaged or married to him, without her parents knowing.

Nargus still tries her best in front of Neelam's parents so they like her son Moeen. Nargus turned her own grandsons against their in-laws even though they had been so nice to them. Nargus made sure her son had a nice life, but she destroyed both her grandsons' lives.

In 1997 at Neelam's wedding, Ajmal Rafiq's daughter was going around telling all the people that she was engaged to her sister-in-law's brother. And everyone in the wedding said, 'Look what she's saying! Ajmal does not even control his daughter'. Everyone knew that what Ajmal's daughter was saying wasn't true. Ajmal's daughter kept forcing the issue.

In England Ajmal's daughter kept phoning her sister-in-law's brother's factory and when he did not come to the phone she would start talking to his friends. He had had enough of this and told his parents to tell her to stop shaming him in front of his friends.

Ajmal's daughter would not leaver her sister-in-law's brother alone. She started stalking him. Ajmal did not know what she was doing as he was too busy making money, but Nargus knew what she was up to and where she was going. She used to keep her in skirts and she would sit in a car with music playing full blast, with her hair down.

Every time Ajmal's daughter stayed in her sister-in-law's house she would ask her sister-in-law's father when he was going to the mosque, and he would say it wasn't time. She would make a face and say 'Go somewhere else then, you are always at home'. That's how Ajmal's daughter would talk to older people.

When Ajmal's daughter saw her father outside her Nan's house in Accrington she would say, 'There's the madman coming to lecture me again'. Her aunt Kiran would be sitting there laughing.

When Fardeen's sister (Ajmal's daughter) was watching Neelam's wedding film with her brother Fardeen in her Nan's house she said to Fardeen 'Look, this is how weddings should be, like our aunt, yours wasn't proper'. What did she mean? Was Neelam more closely related to her than her own brother Fardeen?

When Fardeen was going to come back to Birmingham after Neelam's wedding he went to meet his sister to say goodbye and she did not meet him. Instead she said, 'why should I meet you? Do you listen to me or my nan?' What her nan wanted was for Fardeen to leave his wife.

One day Ajmal's daughter came to stay in her sister-in-law's house and the sister-in-law's parents had gone out. An older, respected person came to the house and Ajmal's daughter said to him 'Uncle, I have such a bad headache, can you have a word with my fiancé, because he doesn't talk to me?' The man said, 'My child, what are you talking about, who is your fiancé?' The daughter nodded towards her sisters-in-law and said 'their brother.' The daughters-in-law were shocked and told her to be quiet. The man said, 'I've known your family for a long time, and nobody told me your brother was engaged'. Ajmal's daughters-in-law were too shocked and embarrassed to say anything, but the visitor realised it wasn't true.

After the fight in 1999 the same man went to Ajmal's daughters-in-laws' father's house and said to him, 'I was worried about you all because your family is so straight and simple, and this is what Ajmal's daughter said to me. I am old and I have seen a lot, but that little girl frightened me the way she talked to me and by saying such a thing without shame. If you take Ajmal's daughter as your daughter-in-law she will eat you alive!'

But Ajmal's daughter felt no shame about what she had said. She just said to her sisters-in-law, 'Wow that man's rich, he's got a big car, has he got any sons?' They were even more shocked to hear this.

Before the fight Ajmal's daughters-in-law thought it didn't matter what his daughter said or did as she was only a child, but now they thought she had the soul of the devil.

CHAPTER TWO

In 1997 Ajmal's daughter accused her sister-in-law's family of doing something bad to her, which was not true. Because she was trying to cover her own tracks, she was afraid her sister-in-law's family would tell her father Ajmal that his daughter had stolen expensive jewellery from their house, and they had caught her doing it and explained to her that it was bad to steal and given her an islamic *kitaab* (book) to read. Ajmal's daughters-in-laws' family weren't going to tell her father Ajmal what she'd done, but what they didn't know was that Ajmal's daughter had accused the family of a bigger crime, which was part of the plan of Nargus and her granddaughter to make Ajmal's daughters-in-laws' brother look bad.

Ajmal's daughter-in-law's family kept Ajmal's daughter so nicely at their house, she said she wanted to call her father. Ajmal's daughter-in-law's family said that of course she could. Instead she called her Nan and said, 'Nan you have no idea what state I'm in and how I have been treated here, you have no idea what's been happening, you will be shocked.' Ajmal's daughter-in-law's family were shocked to hear this lie – what was she talking about?

She then put the phone down and then her father Ajmal's phone rang and she picked it up. Ajmal angrily shouted at his daughter and told her to give the phone to her sister-in-law's father.

But instead she said he wasn't home and put it down. Here sister-in-law's father tried to take the receiver, but she would not let him. She made an excuse that her dad had put the phone down because he had to go out, he was busy. Later we found out that this was all planned and Ajmal was involved with his mother-in-law, they planned it together to make his daughter-in-law's family look bad.

After Feroz Rafiq got married, Nagina and her husband Ajmal again changed, after they heard that their daughter-in-law's brother was going to get married. Ajmal and his wife were angry at their daughters-in-law and were planning revenge.

Nagina sat her sons down and said, 'No matter what happens don't leave your Nan. What she says to you will be for the best.' She meant even if it meant breaking up their marriages.

When Ajmal phoned his daughters-in-law and told them to come to Pakistan, he said, you only have one brother, you should come to Pakistan to your brother's wedding, and he told his daughters-in-law to buy return tickets with their father's money as he couldn't afford it. But when his daughters-in-law got to Pakistan, Ajmal would not let them go to the wedding. Instead he said, 'Has your father written his house to you so you can go to your brother's wedding?'

Ajmal also said to his daughters-in-law that their brother's wife was 'eating' his daughter's right.

When Ajmal called his daughters-in-law to Pakistan there was no one to look after their parent's house, so they let a close friend look after it while they were away. Ajmal kept saying to his daughters-in-law, 'Is that man who is looking after your Dad's house more closely related to your father than me?' He wanted to look after their houses, and his daughters-in-law know what would have happened. He would have taken everything, and tricked them as he had tricked his brother Shahid, by taking his house and selling it.

In 1998, before Ajmal's daughters-in-law and son Fardeen were going to go to Pakistan, Fardeen had no money because he had spent it all on himself. So Ajmal's daughters-in-laws' father paid for their tickets. Fardeen did not have any money to spend in Pakistan, and Fardeen told his wife to get £500 from her father. To this day Nagina is wearing all the expensive clothes she took to Pakistan from England, all from her daughter-in-law's mother's house.

When Fardeen went to Pakistan he didn't pay for his tickets, nor did he have any money to buy clothes for his family abroad.

In Pakistan, Ajmal Rafiq started a fight at his daughter-in-law's brother's wedding because he did not want it to happen. He would not let his daughters-in-law go to their brothers' *mehndi*.

When his daughter-in-law's brother got married in Pakistan, someone came up to Ajmal and said 'You should have put on a big wedding for your son too'. Ajmal got angry and started swearing at him. He fought with the man at the wedding and with his daughter-in-law's parents. He fought with them all through the *mehndi* and on the wedding days. Everyone was talking about it.

When Feroz got married in Pakistan, Nagina told his wife 'Your mother gave gold earrings to all of us for Fardeen's wedding, why hasn't she done the same for Feroz' wedding?' But Nagina's daughter-in-law's mother was not in Pakistan at the time Feroz got married. All Nagina cared about was gold and money.

In Pakistan Nagina said to her daughters-in-law, 'When you got married your father gave you £2000 for your wedding, so where is that money? If you were a good daughter-in-law you would have given it to your in-laws, they come first'.

But what is she talking about? She had already used £2000 from her daughter-in-law's father. If Ajmal's daughters-in-law's father did give money to his daughter it was none of her business. It was her daughter-in-law's money and she would have spent it in her own time, because she knew her father-in-law was not going to settle her in her new house. She knew she would have to do everything herself. What right did Nagina have to that money? Ajmal and Nagina only asked their daughters-in-law's *rishtay* for their money. It just shows how greedy Nagina's family are.

People are saying to Ajmal's daughters-in-law's family that they don't understand why Ajmal says he has a big house in Mirpur. It's just a cramped little house and the walls have big cracks in them. There's nothing so great about it, yet this pile of bricks and cement was worth more to Ajmal than his own grandson.

When Feroz Rafiq got married in Pakistan, Ajmal told the bride's father not to give anything to his daughter because his sister Shiza would not be able to afford to give anything for her daughter's wedding as her husband had just died. She would feel ashamed. Ajmal said he would buy Feroz and his wife what they needed. He knew very well that her father would still give her money over time, but he wanted to be able to say that they hadn't given their daughter anything.

In Pakistan, Ajmal's daughter would see Feroz Rafiq and his wife happy together and start to cry. She would phone her nan Nargus in England and tell her everything. Feroz Rafiq's sister would say to Feroz, 'What kind of brother are you? You are suppose to listen to me and get revenge for me, instead you are keeping your wife nicely!'

In Pakistan Feroz Rafiq's wife told Nagina to explain to her son that he should not hit his wife. But Nagina sat her son and his wife down and said to Fardeen, 'Even if you beat her to death it doesn't matter, that's your right as her husband'. Nagina's daughters-in-law looked very shocked.

Before Fardeen went to Pakistan his in-laws looked after him very well and bought him everything. In Pakistan he wouldn't spend time with his mother but went out all day with his friends and lost a lot of weight. Only on the day before he was coming back to England did he spend time with his mother. He made her feel sorry for him. He put his head on her lap and started to cry and say he wanted to stay longer because he didn't know how he was going to be treated in England. Ajmal's daughters-in-law were shocked at these lies.

Fardeen's wife did not understand why he did not care for his son, but she now understands that it is because he had no love or attention from his own parents when he was younger.

When Ajmal's daughter-in-law's brother was going to get married, Nagina Ajmal said to her daughters-in-law, go and ask for your share of your father's house. They said they didn't want to be horrible sisters to their brother. This made Ajmal more angry. If only he had been a good person, others could not have ruined everything.

We often ask ourselves what possessed Ajmal to do such evil things. Then we remember something that is written in the Q'ran: a person who has no shame can do anything.

If Ajmal was good and wise he wouldn't have been in the mess he had created for himself. It takes a lot of hard work to build a bridge, but it takes just one stupid man to blow it up.

When Feroz was going to come to England, Nagina told him that he should ask his father-in-law for a lot of things and make sure he spent plenty of money on him. She said 'Your father-in-law's money is not only for his son, you have a right to a lot of it as well because you are his son-in-law'.

In Pakistan Nagina borrowed money off her daughter-in-law's mother and used it to buy 35 ready-made suits for her sister-in-law,

Neelam. When Nagina's daughters-in-law were going back to England, she made them carry the suits back to England.

Nagina did not think people would talk about what she gave to her daughters-in-law, which was just two cheap suits. Feroz Rafiq's wife also left her wedding clothes in Pakistan and half her gold, because Ajmal wanted the money.

Ajmal had no money in Pakistan to feed his daughters-in-law when they went there, so he again borrowed money from his daughter-in-law's father. To this day Ajmal Rafiq's daughter-in-law's mother buys them clothes and anything her daughters need.

Nagina would say to her daughters-in-law 'Your brother should not marry somewhere else. It's better if you all marry into one family, otherwise your brother's wife will take my son's right'. But why didn't her brothers marry into the same family as her sisters-in-law?

Ajmal would keep saying to his daughters-in-law that his sons should live together even if they didn't get along with each other. Feroz Rafiq would come home angrily and tell his wife that Fardeen kept fighting with him at his factory and didn't get on with him, but Ajmal would not listen.

Ask Ajmal why he didn't keep his younger brother and his wife in his six-storey house in Mirpur. It is because Nagina doesn't get along with her brothers-in-law. Ajmal used to upset his daughters-in-law by saying to them that wherever he took them people did not really like them. He thinks the whole world is bad apart from his own family, but in fact it's the other way round. Ajmal should look at himself in the mirror.

When Ajmal needs his friends and relatives in England he uses them, and when he doesn't need them any more he pushes them away and bad-mouths them. His daughters-in-law used to say that even their neighbours' dog was treated better than they were.

In Pakistan Ajmal bought a bed for Feroz and his wife and then kept saying, 'Remember I bought you this bed to sleep on. You have to remember it was me that bought it.' But Feroz' wife was hardly going to drag the bed with her all the way to England! Yet Ajmal kept saying this. She had left everything in Pakistan and Ajmal and Nagina were still complaining.

In Pakistan Ajmal's daughter-in-law's aunt was ill with cancer, and Ajmal and Nagina would not let their younger daughter-in-law go to see her. When they returned to England they heard she had died. At the funeral, instead of expressing their sorrow, Ajmal and Nagina started bad-mouthing their daughters-in-law. The daughters-in-laws' aunts were shocked and stared at Ajmal and Nagina. Had they come to mourn or to start a fight?

Ajmal also swore at all his daughters-in-laws' aunts and said 'Your nieces had better give my sons their stays, or all of you will be sorry.' Ajmal and his wife don't care about life or death, only about money and revenge.

When Feroz and his wife were returning to England, Nagina filled their cases with Neelam's ready-made suits. Feroz' wife said, 'How can we carry all this? There won't be any space in the suitcase!' Nagina told her to take some of her wedding clothes out and leave them behind as she would not be wearing them all. So she left all her wedding clothes, including her jumpers and shoes and many of her suits, and Nagina put them all into her daughter's *dajj* (dowry) when she got married.

When Feroz and his wife were coming to England, he phoned his father-in-law and asked him for money for the air fare. With the money Nagina went shopping and bought Neelam and her sister Kiran some ready-made suits, but she bought nothing for her daughters-in-law.

When Feroz' wife came back to England she was very ill and had to stay in hospital. Feroz was very worried about her. Ajmal said in front of her, 'Why are you worrying about your wife so much? You're young, there are plenty of other girls in England, go out and look around'. Feroz said to her 'Ignore my father, he is mad'.

Ajmal told his daughters-in-law that they had not suited his sons because they were too handsome for them. But did Ajmal suit his wife?

He suggested to Feroz' wife that she should take out life insurance while she was ill.

When Ajmal was asking for his daughters-in-laws' *rishtay*, he would take them to Accrington and he and Nagina would say 'We're not like your other relatives, always asking for money. Everyone isn't the same. If you marry our sons we will treat you so nicely that all the world will look.'

Before Ajmal went to Pakistan in 1997 after his son's wedding, he borrowed hundreds of pounds to give his solicitor for his son's stay, and then left it for his daughters-in-laws' father to pay. Ajmal and his mother-in-law both like living on other people's money.

Jamil Rafiq, Ajmal's second son, phoned Feroz' wife from Pakistan to ask her to get her brother to write a sponsor letter for him so he could come to England. Why didn't he ask his Uncle Moeen? Nargus just wanted to use Ajmal's daughters-in-laws' parents' money.

When Ajmal phoned his sons to demand money they would not come to the phone, saying he would never leave them alone.

CHAPTER THREE

Feroz would only work for two weeks at a time and then go off to Accrington and spend it there with Neelam. When he had spent it all he would come back to Birmingham and ask his wife for the money her mother had given her. Why didn't his Aunt Kiran and Uncle Moeen give him money? Ajmal would accuse his daughter-in-laws of taking his sons' money. Don't they have a right to spend their husbands' money?

Ask Ajmal why Nagina is eating his money. Ask him why he was paying for his son Haroon to eat when he was telling Fardeen not to spend a penny on his wife and child. Ask Neelam why she is eating her husband's money and why she isn't letting him send his sister Nagina money in Pakistan. Neelam told Ajmal's daughters-in-law to call her their in-laws, which would mean Nagina is Neelam's in-law as well. Why isn't Neelam sending £100 a week to Pakistan?

Every job Feroz had he would leave and wouldn't go back to work. When his father-in-law asked his boss why he had sacked him, the boss said he always left at 12 noon. The first time he said he had a dental appointment, the second time he said his nan had died. What could he do but sack him? Feroz' father-in-law was shocked on hearing this.

When Nagina was in England she would send her children to her daughters-in-laws' mother's house, then ring her and tell her she had promised them their aunt would buy them some nice clothes. She could not be bothered to buy clothes for her children herself. Ajmal and his wife used the family in any way they could.

When Ajmal's daughter stayed in her sister-in-law's house the daughters-in-law's mother gave three suits and pairs of shoes and £30 in cash. She put the suits in her bag and said, 'Is this all you're giving me? What about my Auntie Kiran and my Nan? You must give them suits too!'

When it was Nagina's son Haroon's birthday Nagina would not buy him clothes. She used to send him to her daughters-in-laws' mother's house so she could buy him clothes.

Ajmal's daughters-in-laws' family like Haroon a lot, but Ajmal and Nagina turned him against them. They had a photo of him, and Ajmal took it back.

When Ajmal and his family first came to England they went to their daughters-in-laws' parents' house and the mother gave his daughter £50 because she had not bought any clothes for her. Ajmal said, 'Is this all you are giving my daughter?'

When Fardeen and his wife came back to England they did not have a washing machine. It was the only thing left to buy, because Fardeen's father-in-law had bought her everything else. So Fardeen's wife phoned her father-in-law in Pakistan and said, 'Uncle, could we keep Fardeen's wages this week to buy a washing machine?' Ajmal got angry and said, 'Here we are sitting starving in Pakistan and you are thinking of buying a washing machine for yourself? Go and take your husband's clothes to the laundry!' But Ajmal had bought a washing machine himself with his son's money when he had stayed in Rochdale. Later Fardeen's father-in-law bought one for his daughter. Ajmal had told his daughter-in-law to take all her clothes to the laundry even though she was seven months pregnant. She could not carry all those clothes all the way there.

When Ajmal's grandson was born he would not let his daughters-in-law spend any money on clothes for the baby. Fardeen's wife begged her husband to buy a cot, so he did so. When Ajmal saw it he shouted, 'Didn't I tell Fardeen not to buy a cot? You have wasted so much money, that money could have come to us in Pakistan. We're the ones who need it!' Ajmal also told her to potty-train the baby at four months and not buy any more nappies!

Feroz' Aunt Kiran told Feroz that she had been happy to spend £100 on dresses for her baby daughter when she was born. Didn't Ajmal think his grandson deserved the same treatment?

Nagina used to phone her daughters-in-law in England and tell them that when their mother was going to buy them clothes they should tell her to give them the money instead and send it to her in Pakistan.

Ajmal's daughters-in-law once caught his daughter writing to a boy. They told her that in Islam it is bad to do such a thing and she should not do it again.

Ajmal's daughter had a best friend who knew every boy in Accrington. They would go to a phone box together and his daughter would put on a false voice and phone her sister-in-law's parents. She would say she wanted to talk to her sister-in-law's brother. Neelam would do the same thing when she phoned Feroz in Birmingham. If his wife picked up the phone she would change her voice and say she wanted to talk to Feroz. When Feroz picked up the phone she would talk to him normally.

When Ajmal's daughter got married in England an older, respected person said to Ajmal that he had heard Nargus had arranged his daughter's marriage and Ajmal had not even known where he was giving his daughter. He had quickly got her married out of the family and out of the caste so that she could come to England.

Ajmal quickly made up an excuse. He said he had known his son-in-law's family a long time ago and his daughter and her husband had been at college together and their eyes met and they fell in love. Ajmal thought what he said was good and he felt proud. The older man knew it was a lie. He shouted at Ajmal and said he had no shame. Ajmal went quiet.

Ajmal's daughter was 14 years old when she went back to Pakistan – she certainly did not go to college in England. And if she had had her eye on someone else, why was Ajmal after his daughter-in-law's brother? What kind of father is Ajmal, shaming his daughter like that? She was not married or even engaged to her sister-in-law's brother and she made such a big deal out of it. Ajmal's daughters-in-law were married, why should they stay quiet about what their husbands had done to them?

If Ajmal's daughter was ashamed in front of everyone because she did not marry her sister-in-law's brother, that is her own fault for going around telling everyone she was engaged when nobody had even asked for her *rishta*.

Ajmal's daughter-in-law's father used to say to Ajmal that he was like a son to him. He did not know that Ajmal wanted to be his only son. He wanted his daughter-in-law's brother out of the way so that everything could be his. He would try to compete with his daughter-in-law's brother. Whatever his daughter-in-law's father gave his son, Ajmal wanted for himself.

No one can afford to give their daughter's *rishtay* to Ajmal's sons because Ajmal would soon have them bankrupt.

When Fardeen got married, Nargus and Kiran did not go to the wedding. Ajmal himself did not do his son's wedding because he was planning to split Fardeen up from his wife after his son's stay in England.

When Moeen got married Ajmal kept telling his daughter-in-law to give clothes to Nargus and Neelam, otherwise it would shame him in front of them. But what did Ajmal's mother-in-law give to Fardeen on his wedding? Nothing!

When Ajmal's daughter-in-law's parents used to go to Accrington, people there used to tell them they were concerned about Ajmal's daughter because she was always out. Ajmal should realise that earning money all the time wasn't as important as being at home with the children.

When Ajmal's daughter got married, none of her own relatives came to the wedding, even though Ajmal cried and begged them. But no one wanted to know Ajmal's daughter because she had accused everyone of doing bad things to her. She had also accused her Dad's sister, who lives in Blackburn, Ajmal's daughter said she had hired boys to kidnap her in a car but she had got away. None of this was true.

It is too dangerous for anyone to let Ajmal's daughter stay in their house, because she just makes things up and tells lies about what people have done to her.

In England Feroz Rafiq's father-in-law bought his daughters everything for their house, including a fridge, washing machine, gas cooker, sofas, drawers, beds and electrical appliances. He didn't even take rent from his sons-in-law. Still Ajmal said this wasn't enough. He said to his daughter-in-law's father, 'I've done two of your daughters and you've only given me enough things for one. Give me two fridges and washing machines!' His daughter-in-law's father said, 'OK let one couple move into the other flat and I'll put everything in it for them as well'. And Ajmal said, 'No, my sons are going to live together because I need the money.'

Really Ajmal Rafiq wanted his daughter-in-law's father to give him extra things so that he could give them to his daughter when she got married. Since Ajmal's daughters-in-law got married into his family, all Ajmal and Nagina talked about was money, and what their daughter-in-law's father should give them. Ajmal would say to his daughters-in-law that he wouldn't say anything to his sons if they did anything wrong, otherwise his sons would turn against him and wouldn't send him money.

All the time Ajmal's mother-in-law and her daughter-in-law Neelam were in Pakistan, Ajmal would phone his daughters-in-law and demand extra money to feed his mother-in-law. Nargus called Feroz to Accrington and told him to phone a man in Birmingham, and arranged to send £1500 to his brother Jamil in Pakistan for his visa.

Nargus told Feroz to tell the man she would pay him in a week. The man sent the money to Pakistan for her, but Nargus then refused to give him his money back. He kept phoning Feroz Rafiq's wife and asking for the money, because Nargus had given him her name and phone number.

Then Fardeen phoned his nan Nargus to tell her to pay the man, and Nargus said that if the man came to get the money she would set the dogs on him. Nargus wanted Ajmal's daughters-in-law to pay her money, but in the end Nargus had no choice. Many months later she eventually had to pay him.

Feroz and Fardeen happily phoned their father Ajmal and told him their father-in-law had brought them many things for their house. Ajmal went quiet and put the phone down. Then he phoned his daughters-in-laws' father's house and said angrily, 'Why are you buying things for my sons? You're trying to take my sons away from me. I'm their father, I will buy my sons what they need.'

Ajmal could not accept that his sons were getting everything straight away and he did not have those things for himself. What kind of father is he who cannot accept his sons' happiness?

Ajmal said to his daughters-in-law, 'I cannot shout at my sons if they do bad things because I am like a friend to them. You tell your husbands yourselves'. And when Ajmal's daughters-in-law told their husbands not to do bad things, Ajmal would quickly turn his sons against their wives by telling them to 'forget the bitches'.

Ajmal's daughters-in-law were shocked at how he had changed. His sons didn't need a friend, they needed a father.

When Nargus phoned her grandson Feroz in Birmingham he quickly took the phone to his room and closed the door to make sure his wife was not listening. When he put the phone down ten minutes later he came out of his room and said to her 'Quickly, phone the ambulance, I have just swallowed 20 paracetamol tablets!'. His wife did not know what was going on. She was shocked and panicked. Feroz was sitting calmly.

When Feroz got to the hospital he was worried because the doctors checked him and shook their heads, then left him. He kept telling his wife to get the doctors to check him quickly. 'They don't care if I die!' he said.

The doctor told her Feroz was just attention seeking and was wasting their time. He would vomit the pills out.

Feroz said to his wife later, 'You always listen to me, don't you. Now that I have taken an overdose we are going to stay at my Nan's house for a few days'. When he got to Accrington he phoned his mother-in-law in Birmingham and swore at her, saying he was not coming back. That's when his wife realised it was all a plan and an excuse to enable him to move to Accrington.

When she phoned her mother-in-law in Pakistan, Nagina could only talk about money. She said 'Forget Feroz, he is stupid. You just book £300 this week and tell him when he sends his father money he should send me my money separately.' That was all she was worried about. She did not even ask how Feroz was.

Nargus told Ajmal's daughters-in-law to move to Accrington to be near her. Why was she asking them to ask their father for £5000? Couldn't Nargus settle her grandsons with her own money if she wanted to keep them there?

Daaj (dowry) only means giving daughters on their wedding day, not for the rest of their lives. Nagina had told her daughters-in-law not to move to Accrington. They were settled in Birmingham and had a house there.

Feroz went to Accrington for a couple of weeks, and when he returned his wife was shocked to see the state of him. His eyes had lines under them and he had lost a lot of weight. Nargus and Neelam didn't seem to think they should be looking after him.

If Nargus had been a good Nan she should have sent Feroz back to Birmingham to his wife. Instead she kept him there and turned him against her.

Kiran said to her nephew Fardeen 'We're your family and you're supposed to listen to us and do things our way'. If Kiran cared so much for her nephews why didn't she bring them from Pakistan herself with her own money? When it was time for her to send money she would put the phone down. Now that her nephews have come to England she suddenly cares about them. Kiran hardly talks to her own husband, she ignores him, unless she needs the dishes washed. She sits with her mother and laughs at her husband, because she knows he is scared of her.

Ajmal tried his best to turn his daughters-in-law's family against their relatives, but his plans backfired. He told them his wife Nagina had had to sell all her gold to have their house in Mirpur built, which was not true. Ajmal only said that because he wanted his daughters-in-laws' family to feel guilty so that his daughters-in-law would give the rest of their gold to Ajmal too.

Ajmal said to his daughters-in-laws' mother 'My house is nearly finished now. How much money do you think my sons should send me? His daughters-in-law mother replied, 'You decide that Ajmal, you must know best because they are your sons.' He replied, 'Still, I want you to tell me how much they should send'. She suggested about £200 a month. Ajmal replied, 'I see, you bitch sisters are all the same, I realise that now. £200 is nothing. It won't be enough for my family.'

Ajmal's daughters-in-law now know that no one can even tell a joke to Ajmal and his family because they take it seriously, remember it and then seek revenge. You can't even write letters to them in Pakistan because they make photocopies and keep them in the hope of blackmailing someone.

Since Ajmal has been coming to England his mother-in-law Nargus has never thought of inviting him to her house to feed him. She doesn't care that he is living in a rented house and doesn't think of cooking a meal for him. Yet she criticises other people for this sort of thing.

Whatever laws Ajmal's sons break, Nargus forwards their fine demands to Ajmal's daughters-in-law's house. How does she think they are going to pay £1000 of fines for them?

Nargus always complains that she is ill, but she is only ill when couples get back together, not when she breaks them up.

Ajmal is going around telling everyone about the crank calls at his daughters-in-laws' house where she is married. He knows Nargus and Moeen are behind them, but he wanted to blame them on his daughters-in-law to make them look bad. When people hear what Nargus did to them, they say she is a sick, unstable old woman who just can't stop destroying other people's lives, and Ajmal is her puppet. She pulls his strings and tells him what to do. He has no mind of his own.

Ajmal would get angry whenever people came to his daughters-in-laws' parents' house. He would say, 'Why have these people come to your father's house? Are they more closely related to your dad than me?' He didn't want anyone else to come to the house, he wanted to be the only one close to the family so that no one else could interfere when he took over everything that belonged to his daughter-in-law's brother.

CHAPTER FOUR

Ajmal said to his daughters-in-law that his sons couldn't feed them all their lives. He did not teach his son that Muslims do not drink alcohol. Feroz knew nearly all the pubs in Accrington and Birmingham and would always come home drunk.

Since Feroz had come to England in 1998 he avoided working. Every job he started, he would soon leave. His Nan Nargus had other plans for him. She told him to take an overdose of pills as an excuse, so that he could come to her in Accrington.

This was when Feroz was living in Birmingham happily with his wife. His father was not happy, which was why he turned Feroz against his wife and her father.

Nargus's and Neelam's phone calls came three times a day, so Feroz kept running off to Accrington. After that Feroz Rafiq changed. he did not want to know his wife any more, and that's when he planned to take the overdose.

When we told Ajmal what had happened he did not care. All he said was, 'Forget Feroz, send me £300'.

At one time Feroz ran off to Accrington after having a fight with his brother Fardeen without telling his wife or her family. All week we looked for him. We could not even tell the police that Feroz had not come home, because Feroz took his father's car and drove it without a licence. When we phoned his Nan Nargus to say Feroz had run off, we found that all along he had been with his Nan in Accrington. Nargus had lied. She has made it hell for my family, and Ajmal helped her.

Nargus and Ajmal are also responsible for Feroz swearing at his father-in-law. In the end Ajmal made his sons beat their wives up, and he made his sons beat their father-in-law.

The reason Nargus kept Feroz in Accrington was so that he could look after her daughter Kiran's children and do their housework for them.

When Feroz Rafiq ran off to Accrington, Nargus would phone her grandson Fardeen and tell him to throw Feroz' wife out and send her back to her mum's house, saying he couldn't afford to keep her. Fardeen replied that he couldn't throw Feroz' wife out of her own house.

Every time Feroz Rafiq's wife phoned Accrington to talk to Feroz, Nargus would say Feroz had gone out. And when Feroz' wife said she would phone again later, she would reply that he wouldn't be home until late. She said it was no good phoning Feroz later because she didn't know what time he would be back. Yet all along he had been sitting right beside his Nan, listening to the conversation.

When Feroz' wife phoned Accrington and told Nargus she should send him back to Birmingham, Nargus would reply that he was staying with her.

Feroz' wife said her in-laws needed money in Pakistan, and Nargus would reply that she didn't care.

Nargus and her daughter-in-law Neelam also told Ajmal Rafiq's daughters-in-laws to forget their real in-laws and to call them their in-laws instead. Nargus would turn Feroz Rafiq against his own mother by saying to Feroz that she did not care about him, because she had left him in Pakistan for five years when she had come to England. She would use that as an excuse to get Feroz on her side. Nargus also had a habit of taking other people's children and turning them against their mother.

Finally when Feroz' wife got through to him and told him to come home, he replied that he would come back and not leave her again only if she gave him £5000 and a Jeep.

From behind the receiver on the other end Feroz' Nan and his Aunt Kiran were both telling Feroz what to say. Kiran was also swearing at Ajmal Rafiq and at Feroz' father in-law, behind the receiver.

Kiran and Nargus were also saying to Feroz. 'You see your wife doesn't care about you, otherwise she would have given you the £5000'.

When Ajmal Rafiq came to England last he said to his daughter-in-laws' father, 'I've been waiting for this moment for a long time. My house is built now and my sons have their stays in England arranged, so now I can finally say this. Your daughters are going to be without their husbands all their lives, because you didn't do my daughter's marriage to your son.'

Nargus had said to her grandson Fardeen Rafiq that if his wife's brother got married to his sister she would split Fardeen up with his wife. She also said that she would do her granddaughter's *rishta* herself, from wherever she wanted to.

When Ajmal was asking for his daughters-in-laws' *rishtay* he used to take them to Accrington, and Ajmal and Nagina would say, 'We're not like your other relatives, always asking for money, everyone isn't the same, if you marry our sons we will treat you nicely and all the world will see.'

Nagina said to Feroz' wife, 'I'm glad you've come to Pakistan and married my son because I was sick and tired of cooking for him, he was asking for two chapatis every morning. Feroz needed a loving and caring mother, but he did not have one'.

When Nargus went to Pakistan she kept going around bad-mouthing Ajmal's daughters-in-laws' brother. But she should look at how bad her own son was. Moeen used to come home drunk all the time, which was the cause of his kidney failure. Nargus should be ashamed of him.

Nargus also tricked Neelam's parents, because she did not tell them Moeen was ill and had kidney failure until after she had got him married to Neelam. They are still angry over this.

Neelam's mother has never forgiven Neelam for marrying out of the family. Now if Neelam the homewrecker is not happy with her own marriage she should bang her head against the wall for not listening to her parents, but that does not mean she has the right to take other people's husbands away.

A few days before Eid, Feroz' wife phoned Nargus and told her to send Feroz back to Birmingham because she wanted to celebrate Eid with him. Nargus refused and said Feroz would celebrate Eid with his Nan. She also said to Feroz' wife that she was just jealous because she did not have a Nan. Feroz' wife was shocked.

As soon as Feroz got back to Birmingham Neelam would phone straight away and say she missed him and wanted him back. Neelam would send Moeen to work and go out with other people's husbands.

Each time Feroz returned to Birmingham he would be in a bad mood and would bang and kick the drawers in his bedroom so that they broke. And he would scrape dirt and mud off his shoes on to the carpet so his wife had to keep cleaning it. And when his wife put food on the table for him he would say 'Leave the food on the table and get out, bitch!' Feroz was doing his best to make his wife fed up with him so that he would have an excuse to leave again and run back to his Nan.

When Feroz went to Accrington, his Aunt Kiran would turn him against his own nephew, Fardeen's son, so that Feroz would like her children more. He would ignore his nephew. Feroz would look at his nephew and say to his wife 'Our Aunt Kiran's daughter is walking now, look at yours, [meaning his nephew] he can't even stand up yet'. Was Kiran's daughter more closely related to him than his own nephew?

Whenever Feroz saw his in-laws walking outside, he would swear and say to his wife in front of his father, 'Look, there's your bitch mother and your son-of-a-bitch father coming into our house.' Feroz' wife was shocked and told Ajmal to tell Feroz not to swear at his mother-in-law. Ajmal would touch the Koran and say his son had not sworn. Feroz' wife said to her father-in-law, 'What are you doing, uncle? Your son is swearing in front of you and you are touching the Koran and saying he is not!' Either Ajmal is very bad or very stupid, we still cannot work out which.

Fardeen told his wife and her family that when his Nan told him to get her a *taveez* she had told him 'When you get it for me remember not to put it in your coat pocket, because your wife might find it.' Nargus was up to her old tricks again, she was up to something bad. She wanted that taveez to do something wicked.

When Feroz' father-in-law came to his daughter's house he would bring meat and chicken and put it in their freezer, which was usually empty. Ajmal would say to his daughter-in-law, 'Your father should put the meat in the freezer and then go straight home, why does he come in and sit down?' But Ajmal's daughters-in-law's father would only sit for a short time to pick his grandson up.

Feroz' mother-in-law used to feel sorry for Feroz when he

couldn't work. She used to say, 'It doesn't matter, if you need money I'll give you some'. She would put £10 notes in his pocket. His father-in-law told him he only had to work a year for his stay in England. After that, if he wanted to do marketing and found it easy, he would get him a van. When Feroz told his Dad Ajmal about his father-in-law buying him a van to do marketing, he would get angry and jealous.

Before Ajmal's daughters-in-law were married into his family Ajmal used to take them to his house in Accrington and he and his wife Nagina would put piles of fruit in front of them. They would say 'We are like your father, we don't care about money. We're not misers. We buy lots of fruit.' It was all just for show.

Before Ajmal's daughters-in-law married into his family he and his wife would say to them, 'We have two houses and we will put one in each of your names, all the mortgage is paid.' He told their parents the same thing so that they would give them *rishtay*. But where are those houses now? Ajmal took the mortgage money from the houses and ran off to Pakistan, yet he is still asking for his rights.

Feroz' wife phoned Nagina in Pakistan and told her Fardeen kept hitting his wife when he comes home from work late at night. And he kept banging the doors and waking the baby up crying. Nagina said, 'You haven't told your father any of this, have you?' Feroz' wife said she thought she should tell her first. 'Well don't tell your father' she said. 'He is old and will worry and become ill.'

Feroz' wife told her that Fardeen smoked 20 cigarettes a day, and asked her to tell him not to in case it made him ill. Feroz' mother said 'Let him smoke if he wants to. He earns money for us, so what if he does smoke? Just don't tell your father about this.' Then she put the phone down.

The next day Ajmal phoned his daughters-in-laws' father and

asked him for £2000. In England when Ajmal stayed in his daughter-in-law's house he paid £5 to their milkman, and told his son when he came home from work. He kept on saying this until Fardeen paid his dad the money back.

Every night Feroz would bring his wife a glass of milk and say 'Drink it all, it's good for you'. She thought he cared for her, but she became more ill every day. Then one day she noticed that the milk had a blue colour. When she asked her husband about it he smiled and said 'It's nothing, just drink it'. This time she refused.

Later she was about to wash Feroz' jacket and found an opened box of rat poison in one of the pockets. She was shocked and asked him what it was doing there. She thought he was trying to end his life. Then he admitted that he had been putting it in her milk every night to kill her. She couldn't believe what she was hearing. No wonder she had felt ill.

Feroz also admitted that his Nan had told him to do it. She would phone Feroz' wife and say 'Aren't you dead yet? You should be dead by now. Now we know why she was saying this.

Before the fight in 1999 Ajmal told his daughters-in-law and sons that he was going to take their television to Rochdale because he couldn't live without a TV. Fardeen's wife said 'Yes of course uncle, it doesn't matter, we'll buy a small TV instead.' Ajmal suddenly got angry at his daughter-in-law and said, 'Look at the bitch, she's dying over a TV. Both you sisters are bitches.' They were shocked at what he said.

When Ajmal last came to England he went to his brother Shahid's house in Accrington and told him he was borrowing his car just to drive around in it. In fact he drove the car all the way to Birmingham. Ajmal was laughing with his sons and saying that Shahid did not even know he had driven the car to Birmingham.

Feroz said, 'Let's drive it all over the place and never mind if it gets scratches on it or breaks down, it's not as if it's our car'. Ajmal and his family don't care about other people's things.

As soon as Ajmal's sons and daughters-in-law moved into their flat, Ajmal started asking for money. When people came to see them they were shocked to hear that they were already having to send money to Pakistan.

'You haven't even settled into your new house yet' they said. 'What kind of in-laws do you have that don't care about their sons? How can they afford to send money to Pakistan?'

Ajmal is going around telling everyone his daughters-in-law were 'eating' his sons' money and that his sons belonged to him, not his daughters-in-law. He angrily said to them, 'I haven't got my sons married to you, I have sold them to you, they are no use to me if they can't earn for me.'

Ask Ajmal why he is earning money for his wife but not for his parents. Does that mean that Nagina is using up Ajmal's parents' right? Is that what Ajmal is trying to say?

Ajmal kept telling his daughters-in-law that in Islam sons are supposed to earn for their parents first and then their wives. But they have read in the Islamic *kitaab* that wives and children come first. If he is following Islam he should first teach his sons that Muslims are not supposed to drink alcohol and he should teach his daughters about Islam. His daughters-in-law already know about Islam, but Ajmal's illiterate family do not. Ajmal has not even touched a *kitaab* all his life, what does he know about Islam?

When Ajmal comes to England he sits in front of the TV all day, commits fraud on banks and tries to make his relatives give him money. Then he goes back to Pakistan and says to people, 'Oh, I worked so hard in England!' Ajmal does not work in England, he just commits fraud and runs back to Pakistan with the money.

Ajmal Rafiq's daughter-in-law's father didn't work for 45 years in a metal factory to feed Ajmal's greed. There is a difference between hunger and greed. But how can a person like Ajmal, who has committed fraud all his life, understand that?

In 1997, before Ajmal went back to Pakistan, his relatives told him that if they had any money left they would help him, but they couldn't promise anything. When Ajmal came back to England he said to them, 'You promised me money, now you have to give it to me!'

In 1993 Ajmal tricked his own brother, Shahid. He sent him abroad to Pakistan for a holiday, saying he would look after his house in England. Behind his back he quickly sold the house. When Shahid came back to the UK he had nowhere to live and he has been renting ever since. He has never forgiven Ajmal for this.

About his older brother-in-law Ajmal said 'I am waiting for my wife's brother to call my wife to England, Then I will take money from him one way or another'. But his brother-in-law doesn't owe him any money.

When Ajmal needs money he gets Fardeen to phone all his relatives and ask them for it – he doesn't do it himself.

Ajmal and his wife have a habit of crying in front of people to make them feel sorry for them so that they give them money.

Ajmal hopes he won't have to pay back the money he owes his daughters-in-laws' father, but he will have to pay it back one day whatever happens.

There is a saying that for evil triumph, it is only necessary for good people to do nothing. For Feroz and Fardeen, it is enough punishment to have Ajmal as their father and Nargus as their Nan.

We should tell Ajmal Rafiq:

You can buy medicine with money, but not a cure.

You can buy friends with money, but not loyalty.

You can destroy things with money, but it will not help you to avoid death.

You can earn fame with money, but not respect.

Nagina and her husband must be proud of what they have done. They have both taken their revenge, even though it has meant destroying their sons' lives.

Feroz used to say to his wife, 'Why should I work? What's the use? My father is going to take all my money anyway, so I won't have anything left.' Ajmal's sons would say to their wives, 'You don't know our father. We know him better. He is never going to leave us alone. He will be asking for money all his life.'

Whenever it was time for Ajmal to give something like gifts to someone, he would get his daughters-in-laws' mother to give him clothes. When she gave him some suits, Ajmal would say to the people he was giving the suits to that they were all from him and Nagina.

Ajmal is now suffering because his bank account in Birmingham is closed to him permanently.

Even the clothes Ajmal and his wife gave at Jamil's wedding for his wife abroad were all from Nagina's daughter-in-law's mother's house.

When Ajmal's daughters-in-law used to go to his little house, his wife and children all had to eat from one plate. They used old-fashioned Pakistani metal plates to eat their food from.

In England Nagina and her daughter used to wear their daughter-in-law's used clothes. She would say she and her daughter did not mind wearing other people's clothes.

As soon as Ajmal's house was built in Pakistan he and his wife thought they were too rich for anyone. When his daughters-in-laws' family gave Nagina and her daughter expensive clothes they would not appreciate them. When the daughters-in-law put food

in front of Ajmal he would look at the designs of the plates a̲
say, 'Can't you buy better dishes than these?' But he himself just
had old metal plates to eat from before his house was built.

When Ajmal's daughters-in-laws' parents went to Accrington,
people living nearby would tell them they were concerned about
his daughter as they had daughters of their own and knew what it
was like. They felt Ajmal should know where his daughter was all
the time and keep her at home rather than sending her out all day.

Later Ajmal's daughters-in-law's father told Ajmal this and said
he should not have left himself open for criticism of this kind – he
should have kept his daughter at home.

Ajmal got his daughter married quickly so that he would not
have to take any more responsibility for looking after her. He did
this before he split his sons up from their wives, because he knew
no one would have wanted his daughter once the truth had come
out. Everyone in Accrington knew how bad she was.

When Ajmal and his wife were going back to Pakistan they
phoned their daughter-in-law's father and said 'We have brought
our daughter home now'. Even when Ajmal's daughter went back
to Pakistan she did not get along with her parents, because she was
used to living with her Nan.

┤APTER FIVE

When Ajmal's sister Shiza's husband died, she got compensation from the people who killed him, but Ajmal kept half of it. He has no shame in taking orphans' money. In England Ajmal bought his nephews 45p T-shirts and laughed, saying 'At least I brought them something'.

In 1999 Ajmal came to England three times, and three times his daughters-in-law bought clothes and shoes with their mother's money for his family in Pakistan. Ajmal's sons would not take their money out of their pockets for anyone else. Instead they would waste it on cigarettes and alcohol and on tea for their friends in the factory and on their girlfriends. They would go to theme parks without telling their wives and that is mostly where Ajmal's sons' money would go. Feroz Rafiq would always keep his wallet with him. In the night he would put his wallet under his pillow and in the morning he would put it in his pocket before going to the bathroom. But still Ajmal is going around telling everyone that his daughter-in-law used to take his sons' money and waste it.

When Fardeen's wife was married into Ajmal's family she did not complain about the hovel she was kept in. They had no hot water, the kitchen was always filthy and the food was often out of date. That was how they kept their daughters-in-law. Feroz said to his wife's mother, 'Why should I come back to Birmingham? You haven't made me a *sheesh mahal* for me to come back to!'

Ajmal's daughters-in-law had hardly any money, and when they did have some they would use it to buy clothes for their husbands. Feroz would boast that they wore clothes from expensive shops like Burtons. His Nan Nargus simply bought Feroz £2 shirts from the market, which was enough to make Feroz happy. Ajmal once had a Burtons credit card which he used to buy clothes which he did not pay for.

After Ajmal tricked his brother Shahid and sold his houses, Ajmal bought a shop for himself. Ajmal also borrowed money from his daughter-in-law's father.

Ajmal claims that his daughters-in-law's family owe him – but what is he talking about? He has destroyed their lives and he is busy worrying about what they are supposed to owe him. All he has given them is nightmares and bruises. But they will pay him back, by giving his name to the immigration office, who can deal with him themselves.

Ajmal is going around telling people Nargus has hired barristers and she will get her grandsons their stays in England. But when she tried to hire a solicitor he would not take her case.

Nargus is saying she will get her grandsons married again for their stays in England. Somebody should tell her to get a dictionary and look up the word 'bigamy'.

After Ajmal had made his sons beat their wives, he sat in his daughter-in-law's brother's ex-wife's relatives' house and refused to apologise. He said he was going to make them suffer for at least three weeks. After that, he said, they would come begging to him to get their daughters back with their husbands.

When Ajmal's daughter was getting married in England, Ajmal

phoned his daughters-in-laws' relatives and told them to make his daughters-in-law come to the wedding, because if they didn't he would not have them back. All Ajmal wanted was to have his daughters-in-law and grandson at the wedding for show.

Neelam told Ajmal's daughters-in-law to call her their in-laws. What is that homewrecker talking about? Ajmal's daughters-in-law don't even know her. She is the one that married out of the family. Ajmal's sister and brother were the in-laws, not Neelam or Nargus.

Nargus will not get away with what she has done. Next time she will think twice about splitting a couple up.

How can Nagina badmouth her daughters-in-law when they have done nothing bad in their lives? Women who are as bad as Nagina and Neelam, who marry of their own choice, try to spoil other people's daughters, who are good, and try to bring them down to their level.

Ajmal's sons were grown men, but Nargus wanted to treat them like kids and send them to work for their Uncle Moeen while he sat at home and at the end of the day gave them only £10 or £15 for all they had done. Feroz Rafiq said proudly to his wife, 'Do you know what my job was in Accrington? To look after my Auntie Kiran's children'. That was indeed his job, and it was his sister's job too when she went to stay with her Nan. Kiran didn't raise her sons herself, she made Ajmal's daughter raise them.

Now that Feroz has come to England Nargus had the same plans for him and his wife. Nargus wanted his wife to look after Kiran's children while Feroz worked for his uncle, to make life easier for her own children. As if Feroz and his wife didn't have their own lives to live!

Ajmal is going around saying he has bought a lot of *daaj* for his daughter's wedding. Well, anyone can buy things for their children with money made from fraud!

Ajmal's daughter-in-law's father has four daughters, but he did not find it a burden to feed them. He was still feeding two of them after they were married into Ajmal's family. Ajmal had only one daughter, yet he was still complaining that he couldn't afford to feed her. He and his wife did not even keep their daughter with them because they found it a burden. When she was still only 15 years old Ajmal was complaining to his daughters-in-law that he had to get her married off and she was a big burden to him. Ajmal has ruined it for his daughters-in-law by breaking up their marriages.

Ajmal understands nothing of family honour and family values. He just follows anyone who smells of money.

Shahid told Ajmal's daughters-in-laws' mother, 'It doesn't matter if my nephews hit their fathers-in-law, it's no big deal.' Of course he would not find it a big deal. He beats both his wife and mother-in-law.

Nagina told Fardeen, 'It doesn't matter if you beat your wife, my son, that's your right as her husband'. Does she say the same thing to her son-in-law? Nargus didn't even teach her children the Koran. Her daughter Kiran only learned it four years ago when she went to Pakistan and she was worried about what people would think if they realised Kiran didn't know the Koran. Nargus should think, how will her soul leave her body when she dies, after all the bad things she has done?

Feroz told his in-laws that he and his wife were both going to Accrington for a few days and he told people he was taking a few days off work. When they went to Accrington Nargus would send Feroz to Kiran's house and say to Feroz' wife, 'Look at your mother-in-law, she doesn't care about buying you new clothes, look at how I've kept my daughter-in-law Neelam. I buy her everything, I've kept her so nicely'. She was trying to start a fight and to turn Feroz' wife against her mother-in-law Nagina, but her plan backfired. Feroz' wife did not reply, and Neelam went and sat beside her and said 'Your father-in-law Ajmal is not a good man. He doesn't let you live well. All he cares about is money'.

Feroz' wife looked shocked and said it wasn't like that at all, but Neelam carried on. She said 'Your father-in-law is greedy, isn't he?' Feroz' wife said nothing. Then Nargus nodded to her daughter-in-law Neelam, who got up and switched off the tape recorder that had been running. Feroz' wife was shocked to realise she had been recording the conversation.

When Feroz came back from Kiran's house he was in a very bad mood and would not talk to his wife properly. Later his mother-in-law phoned to ask him when he would be coming back home as he had taken so many days off work, and Feroz said he was not coming back.

'Who have I got in Birmingham?' he said. 'I've decided to stay in Accrington. Send all the rest of my clothes here too.'

'What are you saying, Feroz?' said his mother-in-law. 'You haven't even talked about this, you just ran off. The people at your work say you never told them you were taking time off, they want to know when you are going back.'

Feroz said, 'Don't talk to me like that. Why should I tell you anything? You haven't made a *sheesh mahal* for me to come back to.'

She replied, 'Your brother Fardeen is working on his own and sending money to Pakistan, but he can't do everything on his own. He has a wife and a son to look after.

'What can I do about it? It's not my problem' said Feroz. 'I'm not earning for my father, he doesn't need money, he has enough money. I've got my own life to live, I don't have to send him money all my life.'

His mother-in-law said, 'At least come back to Birmingham and we'll talk about this. Then you can decide where you want to live. Right now your father needs money and Fardeen cannot do everything on his own.'

Feroz got angry and said 'Don't tell me what to do, I'm not coming back to Birmingham! Who wants to stay near your family? After all you are a bitch!' His wife looked shocked and told him not to swear at her mum like that. He replied 'I'll swear whenever I feel like it, you and your mother are both bitches!'

His wife tried to take the receiver from him and he pushed her and hit her. Nargus and her daughter-in-law were sitting there pleased that Feroz was not getting along with his in-laws and wife.

Ajmal's daughters-in-law know plenty of people are bad-mouthing them, but those people should look at their own families and fear the wrath of Allah, because they don't know what their own futures hold yet.

Ajmal cannot hide behind his father Raja Azhar and say what nice people they are. How dare he compare himself with his father? Raja Azhar is a decent and honest man. In England old people still remember him. They called him Truthful Azhar because of his honesty. How is Ajmal going to be remembered?

As for Nargus, with which face does she swear at Raja Azhar when everyone remembers her as a homewrecker?

Ajmal kept phoning his sons to ask for money, yet he had done nothing for them. Fardeen would say, 'I have been working for my father since I was 11 years old by doing marketing for him, but he won't leave me alone. He still keeps asking for money.'

Nargus was angry because people were saying nice things about Ajmal's daughters-in-law and not about her own daughter-in-law, Neelam. That is why she got revenge on Ajmal by destroying his daughters-in-laws' lives. Ajmal and Nargus blackmail each other to get what they want. They both deserve each other, they are both the same.

Neelam also told them that they were not good Muslims. How could she say that? If she had said it to anyone else she would have got a slap in the face.

CHAPTER SIX

Kiran swears at her husband and makes him wash dishes. Is she a good Muslim? Neelam would not listen to her parents and got married where she wanted. As soon as she got married into Nagina's family she made her husband fall out with his older brother. She wore jeans and a T-shirt to college. Is she a good Muslim?

Kiran's husband told his wife not to go to her mother's house because she would do *taveez* on them to make them fight each other. Kiran said she was prepared to leave him, but not to break up with her mother. Is she a good Muslim?

Nargus prays *namaz* (her prayers), and she is still using *taveez* to split couples up. She swears at her elders. She told her older son to leave his wife and get custody of their children. Is she a good Muslim?

Ajmal's daughters-in-law could not even talk in their own house when Ajmal was staying there. He would try to make them angry by saying horrible things about them so that he could record their voices, but they stayed quiet. That made him more angry. What right did he have to hide little tape recorders around their house to record their voices and try to blackmail them?

Nargus claimed she couldn't come to Birmingham because she was ill, but she managed the journey to Pakistan without problems. She makes excuses not to go to Birmingham because she is not happy about her grandsons getting back together with their wives. She also has other reasons, because she has a bad reputation there. Everyone has been talking about what she has done to their families. When she lived in Bevington Road a couple of decades ago she used to use her *taveez* to cause fights between couples, until people had had enough and ganged up on her and she moved to Accrington. But now all the world can see what she is like. She will be remembered there as a homewrecker and a woman who does black magic. God will show her the error of her ways one day.

When Fardeen did bad things in Accrington, people would say, 'Doesn't your Uncle Moeen shout at you when you do something wrong?' He would say 'How is he going to tell me off when I know about the bad things he has done?' Both uncle and nephew would blackmail each other to get away with their wrongdoings.

In Pakistan, Feroz Rafiq took one of his dad's deodorant sprays for himself to use before he came to England. When Ajmal came himself to England he saw his spray in his sons room and quickly seized it from him.

When Ajmal was staying in his daughter-in-laws' house he would look all around the house, and if there was a single toy on the floor he would quickly phone his wife Nagina in Pakistan and tell her that the house was in a mess. Even if someone farted he would go and phone his wife and quickly tell her. He has no shame.

Ajmal sent Feroz Rafiq's wife to buy some chicken and bananas for him. But in England no Pakistani woman goes to a chicken shop. Ajmal did not care. Ajmal's sons were home that day and they would not go themselves. Feroz' wife only had £3 because that was all Ajmal and his sons would give her. She bought the chicken, but she did not have enough money to buy the bananas. Ajmal said it was OK, but later after the fight he went round telling everyone she had bought him chicken but refused to buy him bananas. He was told, 'Why did you send your daughter-in-law to a chicken shop in the first place? You should have sent your sons!' Ajmal went quiet and looked ashamed.

When Ajmal last came to England he told his daughters-in-law that he had told Nagina his daughters-in-law were bitches and no one would blame his sons if they left them.

Ajmal sat angrily in his daughters-in-law parents' house and said 'It serves you right what has happened to your son's marriage, I was wishing for this to happen. I'm glad your son and his wife have split up. I told my daughters-in-law that your daughter-in-law will not stay in your house. You deserve everything that has happened to you.'

Ajmal's daughters-in-laws' parents were shocked and stayed quiet. That made Ajmal more angry. He got up and went to the door and Feroz Rafiq's wife went after him. She said to her father-in-law, 'Come back in uncle, we know you didn't mean to say what you just said, we won't take it seriously'.

Feroz' wife gently tapped Ajmal on the shoulder and told him to come back in. Ajmal turned and said, 'Did you see that? Your daughter just held me by the neck and dragged me in!'

Ajmal's daughters-in-laws' parents were shocked at this lie. They had seen with their own eyes that nothing like that had happened.

Once Ajmal's house was built in Pakistan and his sons were about to get their stays in England, Ajmal and his sons thought they were too good for anyone. They would tell their wives, 'Your place is to sit on the floor while we sit on the sofa'. They forgot whose house they were living in.

The only time Ajmal would pick his grandson was up was for filming and photographs. He kept him just for show. When people were not looking he would ignore him. Ajmal would say he wouldn't give anything to his grandson until he is old enough to know it is being given to him – that way he will earn for him when he grows up.

Ajmal would pick up a bottle of shampoo in his daughters-in-laws' house and say, 'You should not have bought this. The money should have gone to Pakistan'. But he would buy expensive shampoos for himself and his family. This sort of statement would drive his daughters-in-law mad.

One day when Ajmal's daughters-in-law went shopping for groceries they did not have enough money, so they told the shopkeeper they would pay for the rest later. They gave Ajmal the receipt and told him how much they owed, and he said it was his OK. But then he went running to their parents' house and told them his daughters-in-law had cut off the top of the receipt so he did not know what they had bought. He did this to try to get them into trouble. His daughters-in-law explained that the receipt was just as the shopkeeper had given it to them.

Ajmal used to force his son to work overtime in the factory to earn extra money for him. Once Fardeen worked 24 hours and was so tired when he came home that he took his anger out on his wife and child. One day he cut his finger in the factory and did not go to work the next day. Ajmal was angry and said 'Tell my son Fardeen he should have let his finger get chopped off, that way he could have claimed for compensation money and sent it to me in Pakistan'. He told his daughters-in-law to tell Fardeen to go to work just the same to earn more overtime. Nagina complains that her sons are not being treated well by their in-laws, but it is her own husband and her mother who are making it hell for them.

In Pakistan Nagina Ajmal would try her best to turn her daughters-in-law against their parents by telling them they didn't care about them. But their parents had kept them well all their lives – that's what Nagina could not take. She was trying to take revenge on her daughters-in-law because her own mother hadn't cared for her.

Ajmal's daughters-in-law used to tell him he should be happy that his sons listened to him and he should teach them the right way to live their lives. Ajmal would say, 'If I taught my sons the right way then they wouldn't have done fraud for me. This way is better.'

When Feroz and his wife went to stay in Ajmal's house in Rochdale she opened a drawer in the kitchen and found a beer can. She was shocked, but Feroz was smiling at her and his father.

Ajmal Rafiq kept trying to make his sons send him £250 a week. Of course they could not afford to send that much money as they had bills to pay, but Ajmal would not listen. He would swear at his sons and his daughters-in-laws and say, 'Who pays bills? There are other ways. You can do fraud.' He also told his sons to buy less groceries, to save money.

Ajmal and Nagina said to their daughters-in-law that if they were good daughters-in-law they would not use the gas in their house, even in winter, but should send all the money to Pakistan.

Ajmal would phone his mother-in-law Nargus and ask her for money, and she would put the phone down when she heard his voice. Nargus would say to Ajmal 'Why should I give you money? Go and ask your daughter-in-laws' father for money. Say to him that you won't treat his daughters nicely if he does not give you money.'

Once Feroz' wife told Ajmal that Feroz had to work to stay in this country, that's how the law was, and Ajmal would get angry and tell his daughter-in-law not to threaten him.

Shahid said, 'So what if my nephews send £100 a week to Pakistan? They should send money, everyone does'. If he finds it so easy to send so much money, why isn't he sending it to his family every week? He has his own retail business and he has only one daughter, but he still complains that he can't afford to pay the bills or feed his daughter.

Ask Ajmal why he married his sons off if they can't feed their wives. He only got them married to earn money for him in England.

Everyone should indeed send money to their in-laws in Pakistan, but they should not be expected to send every penny and leave themselves with nothing.

Ajmal's son Jamil phoned Feroz' father-in-law, and asked him to get his son to write him a sponsor letter and call him there now, and send him a ticket. Ajmal's daughter-in-law's father said, 'How can my son send a sponsor letter? He has just come back from Pakistan. He has to look for a job again.' Jamil said 'Well tell him to get out and find a job quickly!' What was he talking about? He wasn't even married from the family and he was bossing Feroz' father-in-law. It was Jamil's Nan who wanted to call Jamil to England, so why couldn't she write a sponsor letter? After all Jamil was going to live with her in Accrington.

Ajmal's daughters-in-law did not know that any Muslims drank alcohol until they met Ajmal's and Nagina's family. Feroz would come home so drunk he couldn't get up the stairs. His wife used to have to drag him up. He would stink of alcohol and vomit in the toilet. Ajmal's daughters-in-law were worried that if Fardeen saw his older brother drunk and getting away with it he would start to copy him.

Feroz would say to Ajmal about his wife's family, 'These sons of bitches are so easy to use to come to England. Somebody else can have a go at using them too'. But he was wrong, because they have made sure no one will use them like that again.

Ajmal would bring one of his friends to his daughters-in-laws' house and make them feed him three times a day for three weeks. Then he would shame them by saying horrible things about them in front of his friends.

Nargus would try to record Ajmal's daughters-in-laws' voices on the phone. She would tell them he was not a good man, and swear at him and then edit out her voice from the recordings. But his daughters-in-law stayed silent, so this did not work. This made Nargus angry.

Ajmal tells people that his daughters-in-law phoned his son-in-laws' parents' house and swore at them, which is not true. It was Ajmal who was doing that. Ajmal is the one who kept telling his sons to make nuisance calls to their house. In fact it was his daughters-in-law who had to change their phone number because they had so many calls.

When Ajmal's daughter got married in Pakistan, Nargus and Neelam had a quarrel with Ajmal's son-in-law and Neelam came crying back to England. After that, Nargus told Ajmal to leave his son-in-law and his family. But Ajmal said, 'How can I leave them when my daughter is married there?'

When it was her brother's *mehndi*, Fardeen's wife stayed only one night in her parents' house in Pakistan. Ajmal's daughter-in-law came back to her in-law's house in Mirpur the next day and Ajmal and Nagina were in a bad mood. They got Fardeen to shout at his wife. Ajmal's daughter said 'Look at that bitch, she keeps running to her brother's *mehndi*, she's married now so she should stay in her in-laws' house'. Ajmal's daughter would call her sister-in-law a bitch whenever she felt like it. What right did she have to do that?

Ajmal's daughter would act like a woman of 50 even though she was only 13. She used to order people around and swear at them. She behaves like her Nan Nargus, and she even looks like her.

Feroz used to like and respect his father-in-law and brother-in-law, but Ajmal and Nargus brainwashed him and turned him against them so badly that one day Ajmal made his sons beat up their wives and father-in-law up. Feroz slapped his father-in-law across the face and karate-kicked his sister-in-law several times in the stomach. He also hit his wife hard on the head twice. He was so violent that day that he didn't care who he was hitting. Everybody in the street heard his daughter-in-law's screams. Is it worth giving Ajmal's sons their stays after everything he and his wife put the family through?

Ajmal has also been going round telling people he had been many times to his daughters-in-laws' parents' house to apologise, but he has not even been once. All he had to do was go along with Nargus, but he says 'Why should I apologise to my daughter-in-law's family? My mother-in-law will get my sons their stays'.

As soon as Ajmal comes to England he forgets his religion. He and his sons drink in pubs and flirt with women. Ajmal drinks alcohol and has taught his sons to drink it too. He took the compensation money his sister received from the people who killed her husband. He has made fools of his sons by breaking up their marriages. Ajmal knows nothing about family honour, family values or caste. Wherever he smells money, that's the way he runs. Ajmal shamed his daughter on her wedding day by claiming she was marrying someone she had met without being introduced. Ajmal is Nargus's puppet and she pulls his strings.

Nargus says she can't come to Birmingham because she has a sugar problem, but it hasn't stopped her from going to her granddaughter's wedding in Pakistan. She just doesn't like her grandsons getting back with their wives.

Nargus has lived like a tramp all her life. As soon as her son

Moeen became ill and received compensation, Nargus had her house made new to show off how rich she was. Ajmal did the same thing. People like Nargus and Ajmal do not appreciate what they have. They will get no happiness from trying to destroy other people's happiness.

Nargus will always be remembered as a homewrecker and a woman who practises witchcraft. She encourages her children to go out and look for their own husbands or wives. She turned her daughter-in-law against her parents and made her run away with her son Moeen before she was married to him. She tricked Neelam's parents by not telling them her son was ill with kidney failure until they were married. She teaches her children and grandchildren to go to people's houses and steal from them. She uses other people's money to get her grandsons to England.

Neelam married out of the family and out of the caste without her parents' approval. Even now that she is married, she is still chasing her husband's nephew, Feroz.

Kiran whispers behind her husband's back and only talks to him to tell him to wash the dishes. Because her own marriage has not worked out, she breaks up other people's marriages.

Nargus' daughter Kiran entered this country on someone else's passport. She had pretended she had just come back from a holiday abroad. Ajmal had helped her to enter the UK because he has a big hand in the making of false British passports. If anyone checks in the records, there is no record of her living in the UK, so she is now living in the UK fraudulently.

Afterwards Ajmal somehow got her a passport with her name on it. Ajmal was also planning to call his youngest son Haroon on his daughter-in-law's son's passport (Fardeen's son's passport), but luckily Fardeen's wife did not give him the passport. She was against it and did not agree.

Ajmal and his mother-in-law swear all the time, even though they say they do not.

When Ajmal's children were little he used to send them round to other people's houses to spy on their families and then come back and tell him what they had seen.

Nargus phoned Feroz' wife and said to her 'If you were a good person you would have gently wrapped Ajmal's grandson up and brought him to me. Forget his mother.' But no one would send their baby 100 miles to another town, and Nargus cannot be trusted. She hates Ajmal's daughter-in-law and just wanted to split up her marriage. What did she want the baby for?

Ajmal and his wife like to share their children with others because they don't want to take any responsibility for them.

When Ajmal's daughter was in England she used to stay with her Auntie Kiran, and if someone came to her house who she did not like she would get Ajmal's daughter to bad-mouth them and sit behind her and laugh.

Ajmal and his wife did not teach their sons that they should wash their hands before eating. Fardeen would come home from the factory with oily black hands and his hair and clothes would smell of cigarettes all the time. Wherever he touched the doors he would leave black marks.

Nargus proudly tells people how she brought up her grandsons, and so does Ajmal. But they haven't even taught their children to wash their hands.

Feroz would tell his wife and sister-in-law not to give money to Fardeen because he just spent it on cigarettes. He said he had looked in his locker at work and found 30 boxes, and he was smoking 20 a day. He said he had told Fardeen that he would tell his wife about it if he didn't stop, and that because of this Fardeen had turned everyone in the factory against him.

Fardeen's wife then shouted at him to stop fighting with Feroz and get along with him. She told Feroz that as he was the older brother he should sort out Fardeen's wages and decide how much to send to Pakistan. After that Feroz handled Fardeen's wages. When Fardeen's wife needed shoes she asked Feroz for £20, and Feroz' wife gave her the money. Feroz got angry and demanded it back in his pocket by the end of the week. So Feroz would not work himself but he would take his brother's money and spend it on himself.

Feroz told his Dad that he only took his wife to the shops with him so that she could carry the heavy grocery bags, and accused her of wanting to waste money by buying a bar of chocolate.

When Feroz first came to England and went to his Nan's house in Accrington, he left without telling her and came running back home to Birmingham at midnight. He said to his wife, 'Don't ever send me back their again'. He had had a big argument with his Nan, though she still does not know what it was about.

Every time Feroz went to Accrington his Nan would keep turning him against his mother. She would keep saying to Feroz that his mother never cared for him. Nargus would make Feroz feel worse.

When Feroz came back to Birmingham he would say to his wife, 'Your mother cares for your brother a lot, what is wrong with my mother? Why didn't she care for me?' He would keep saying this because his Nan kept putting bad thoughts into his head.

Feroz Rafiq's wife would tell Feroz that his mother did care for him. She never once turned Feroz against his mother.

Nargus and Neelam kept making Feroz fight with his wife. Nargus would say to him, 'Your dad didn't care for you. He used to kick you around when you were a kid and I used to take care of you. Once I even slapped him for treating you like that.' Feroz would laugh. Nargus would try her best to turn Feroz against his father, and she succeeded.

Nargus would tell Feroz that she could not split Jamil up from his wife as they had a daughter, but she could call him to England get him married again.

When Ajmal's daughters-in-law tell people in England how Nargus split them up with their husbands, people remember how bad she and her daughter were. The woman always had plucked eyebrows, and people are saying she uproots people the way she uproots her eyebrows.

Fardeen told his wife and her family that his Uncle Moeen had called him to his house to help him move some furniture from his bedroom. When he was doing this he saw a big stone with lots of *taveez* tied to it. He asked his uncle about it and Moeen said it belonged to his mother and he should forget about it. Moeen quickly took Fardeen out of the room.

Nargus is going around telling people that Ajmal's daughters-in-law treated her grandsons badly and kept throwing them out of their house. Ask her how she treated her own husband! Does she think everyone has forgotten? People are still talking about it.

Nargus has lived like a tramp all her life. When her son Moeen got ill and was given a lot of money, she used it to have her house renovated and showed it off to her grandson Feroz.

When Ajmal worked in a bank in Pakistan, he used to take people's money and use it for himself. His daughters-in-law and their family should have stayed away from them instead of mixing with a bunch of thieves.

Ajmal also tricked an old woman who was a widow. All her life she had been saving money for her only son. When Ajmal found out he told her she shouldn't leave her money lying around the house as it was not safe. He told her he worked at a bank and would put her money in the bank for her. She trusted him and gave him the money, and instead of putting it in the bank he used her money. When the old woman found out she cried that all her life she had saved for her son. She cursed Ajmal and then she died.

When Kiran brought possessions such as jewellery from Pakistan for people, she would keep half of them herself. Now we know who Ajmal's daughter takes after – her Auntie Kiran. They are both thieves.

Ajmal had some family letters about his sister Shiza and her daughter. He told his son Feroz to keep them in case they could be used to blackmail Shiza. Fardeen's wife said in a letter to her in-laws that her husband was hitting her and didn't get along with Feroz at work. Ajmal kept the letter and told his daughter-in-law that he had made copies and would show them to her husband. But she said she had already told Fardeen about the letter, so the blackmail didn't work.

Ajmal wanted to blackmail Shiza in case she complained about how her daughter Mariam was being treated by her husband Jamil. He had it all planned out. He told his daughters-in-law that his younger sister wanted her son to marry his daughter. 'Why should I give my daughter away to them?' he said. I can't feed my nephews all my life'.

In Pakistan Feroz told his wife not to sit with his parents and his sister. She did not understand why, but she does now.

When Feroz and his wife came to England, Ajmal said to his daughters-in-law that he had fed them in Pakistan and now they owed him.

'You are not my responsibility' he said. 'Go out and work to feed yourself!'

When Ajmal's daughters-in-law were going to decorate the

house, Nargus would phone him and tell him and say they were wasting his money. Then Ajmal would phone and shout at them. Nargus also had her eye on the furniture Ajmal's daughters-in-law's father had provided. She told Feroz to bring the furniture with him from Birmingham to Accrington. How do Nargus and Ajmal feel now that this has all come out?

Feroz' wife's parents sent a parcel every year to their only granddaughter in Pakistan, who is deaf and dumb. Ajmal said angrily to his daughters-in-laws' parents 'I hear a parcel went to Pakistan containing shoes for your granddaughter'. What business was it of his? His daughters-in-law used to send suitcases full of clothes for his daughter every time he came to England, so why was he jealous?

Ajmal has borrowed money from banks in his sons' names. This is one reason why he wants them to get back with their wives. But why did they go and badmouth their daughters-in-law in Mirpur?

Ajmal and his wife asked for *rishtay* for their sons from several houses in England for their sons' stays, but nobody would give them any. Now Ajmal only wants his sons back with their wives so they can stay in England.

Once he had had his house built in Pakistan and his sons had somewhere to stay in England, Ajmal was going to break up their marriages anyway. A few years later he would take them to Pakistan and show them off to rich people, saying they were British and asking for their *rishtay*.

Whenever Ajmal saw his daughter-in-law's parents and their big house he would get angry. He would also get angry when he saw them giving everything to their son, because he could not do the same for his sons. He is the kind of person who is never happy for someone else to be happy. He has to spoil it for them.

He said to his daughters-in-law, 'You're from a village in

Afzalpur, and everyone from there is illiterate.' He thought he was big and clever because he had a big house, but it takes more than just having a big house to be a big man.

Ajmal's wife and children were not hungry, they were just greedy. There is enough in this world for everyone's need – but not for everyone's greed.

Ajmal's daughters-in-law have not opened a visa office to give everyone their stays in England.

When Ajmal Rafiq and his wife went back to Pakistan, Nargus told her grandson Fardeen to get her a *taveez* that she had ordered and give it to his wife's brother. But Fardeen did not listen to his Nan and told his wife's family what she had said. After that Nargus did not like Fardeen.

Nargus then phoned Ajmal's daughter-in-law's parents and said Fardeen was no good and they should forget him and send him back to Pakistan. She said he was like his father. She said Feroz was better then Fardeen, he listened to her and should be sent to Accrington.

When Ajmal Rafiq's daughter-in-law's parents phoned Ajmal in Pakistan and told him what his mother-in-law had said to Fardeen, he told them to keep it quiet. Ajmal then phoned Fardeen and shouted at him for telling his wife and her family about what his Nan had said.

The day Feroz and his wife were coming to England, Ajmal phoned his daughters-in-laws' parents and told them to cook for them. But instead of taking his daughter-in-law to her mum's house, Ajmal quickly took her to his mother-in-law, Nargus. Then he told her to phone her father. When her father asked his daughter where she was and said the food was getting cold, Ajmal jumped up and snatched the phone. He said, 'It's none of your business where we are, your daughter is my daughter-in-law and I can take her wherever

I want!' Nargus and her daughter Kiran were sitting there laughing.

Ajmal kept telling his daughters-in-law that they should have a phone in the house. Kiran does not have a phone, so when her husband wants to phone someone he has to go to Moeen's, where they will all be watching him. Then they check the bill to see where he phoned. They control his every movement. Ajmal's daughters-in-law didn't want a phone in the house because they knew if they did, Nargus would use it to split them up with their husbands. Of course she has done this anyway.

Kiran was going to pay £50 to scrap her car because it didn't work any more. Instead Ajmal said 'Give me £50 and I will get rid of it for you'. But he knew what was wrong with the car. He quickly fixed it and drove it to Birmingham. He laughed about it with his sons and told them he had tricked Kiran.

Ajmal then gave the car to Feroz to drive. When Kiran found out she had been tricked she was very angry, so to get revenge she phoned Feroz and called him to Accrington. When he got there he took the car and drove it around until the insurance ran out and he couldn't afford to reinsure it. Then Neelam and Kiran offered him £100 for the car. Ajmal went crying to his daughter-in-law's house and said Neelam and Kiran had tricked Feroz, because the car was worth at least £500. First they had made Feroz clean it out, then they had bought it from him.

When Ajmal's sons beat their wives up and left, his daughter-in-laws' mother phoned his brother Shahid and told him. He answered, 'So what? I beat my wife up all the time, what's the big deal?' We should tell Shahid that the Prophet had four wives and never raised his hand against any of them. People like Shahid and Ajmal give Islam a bad name.

The family heard that after the fight Shahid went to

Birmingham to collect Feroz and angrily accused Ajmal of starting it. But why isn't Shahid keeping Fardeen in his house? Why has he thrown him out? Can't he afford to keep him, or is that he doesn't trust his own nephew in his house?

After Fardeen's wedding Ajmal said he had only been using his cousin Sheroz because he needed him for the wedding. After that he was going to throw him out. Ajmal's daughter-in-law's mother was shocked and said 'What are you saying Ajmal? Shahid has been really nice to you and helped you a lot.' Ajmal said, 'How do you know he is nice? You don't know anything about him. He owes me money.' But this was not true.

When we heard how Ajmal was shamed in front of his daughters' mother-in-law, we sent this poem to his family:

Hey diddle diddler
Solve this riddler
Of Mr Naqli (fake)
The money fiddler

The bull that tried to reach the moon

The wide-nosed bull
Thought he'd try his scheming plan
And all this happened in Pakistan.
The day his precious daughter was to marry
He thought he'd ask for what he wanted in a hurry
He tried to con his son-in-law's mother
Because he thought she was innocent like the others
Eight thousand pounds is what he asked for
She replied, say that again and we're out of that door

And if you want to sell your daughter
No one will buy her, even for a quarter
Go and sell her somewhere else, she said
You can go and con someone else instead
There are plenty of marriages for my son
And that could easily be arranged and done
I will not beg and go down on my knee
I'm doing you a favour, as you can see
Hearing that the bull's mouth had shut
Must have felt like being punched in the gut.

CHAPTER SEVEN

Before the fight in June 1999 Ajmal Rafiq had told his son Fardeen to lend him £3000 from the bank, because he needed the money for his daughter's wedding. Ajmal did not want to use his own false name to loan money from the bank, so he used his son's name. It just shows what future Ajmal's sons would have had if they had stayed in England.

When Ajmal's daughter got married in England none of her own relatives came to her wedding. Ajmal cried and begged one of his relatives to come. His brother Shahid did come, but he only stayed for 10 minutes. His sister quickly ran off to Pakistan, and you can't blame her. No one wanted to know Ajmal's daughter, because she had falsely accused everyone of doing bad things to her.

Ajmal used every relative in England. No wonder his relatives don't want to know him.

His daughters-in-law should have known better than to get involved with a family of snakes and scorpions who are always ready to bite and sting, because it is in their nature to do so.

Ajmal has now got his daughter married off, but he is still after his daughter-in-law's brother. He keeps phoning their relatives and telling them to tell his daughter-in-law's parents to get their son married from among their relatives, not out of the family. He is still worried about his son's right. But it is none of his business where his daughter-in-law's brother gets married.

Ajmal Rafiq has also been going around telling people that his daughters-in- law used to make his sons sleep outside and did not feed them, yet demanded rent from them, but none of this was true. In England nobody makes anybody sleep outside.

When Nagina was in England her son Haroon used to make tea by using the hot water tap. He used to put a tea-bag in his cup and then fill it with hot water from the tap.

Nagina Ajmal had no time to feed her children, so she used to send them to other people's houses. And talking about rent, Ajmal is the one who used to take rent off his old uncle in Accrington, when he let him stay in one of his houses.

Again, whatever Ajmal Rafiq and his wife do themselves they blame other people for. When Ajmal stayed in his daughter-in-law's house, all he would do was search the house and look in their drawers, but what he was looking for we still do not know. Ajmal would also phone Pakistan twice a week, and he left phone bills of over £300 for his daughters-in-law to pay.

Ajmal Rafiq would also tell his sons to send him money, but Feroz Rafiq refused to work and kept running off to Accrington.

Then Nargus Siddiq's phone calls would come to Fardeen to visit her in Accrington. Half Fardeen's wages would be spent on his train tickets there. Fardeen's Nan would never come to Birmingham herself, she would say she couldn't afford to come on a train. And Ajmal Rafiq's daughters-in-law said to Nargus that they couldn't afford to come on a train either because their in-laws needed the money in Pakistan, and only Fardeen was working.

Nargus would get angry and put the phone down, and then she would phone Ajmal, who would phone his daughters-in-law and shout and swear at them.

Ajmal said to his daughter-in-law's mother, 'Aren't you ashamed of yourself? My daughter's getting married and you didn't make any *daaj* for her'. About his grandson, Ajmal called him a 'spare person' and said his son's money was being wasted on his tins of food and nappies.

Ajmal was planning to come to England and take his brother's shop by buying half of it from his partner and then kicking him out. He only sold the shop to his brother in the first place because he could take it from him when he came back to England.

Ajmal and his mother-in-law were planning to call Jamil Rafiq to England on his brother Fardeen's passport, and send Jamil's wife back to her mother's house, but the plan backfired. Nargus Siddiq was not happy with any of her grandchildren's marriages and was planning to break them up.

But Ajmal and his mother-in-law fell into the grave they had dug for others.

Ajmal told his daughters-in-law that his wife was upset and crying because her mother Nargus went to Pakistan and bought expensive clothes for Neelam, yet she did not think of buying her own daughter a pair of chappels.

Ajmal said that Nargus had said to his daughter after she got married, 'Remember when you go to England that you will live there the way we tell you to live'. Ajmal's daughter replied 'No Nan, you spoiled it for me before with my sister-in-law's family by cutting off my way to England. You are not going to do it again by splitting me up with my husband'.

Nargus got angry. Ajmal also said that in Pakistan Neelam kept bossing his son-in-law about and telling him what to do and who to talk to. His son-in-law said angrily to Neelam, 'Who are you to tell me what to do and try to control my life? Who gives you the right?' Neelam then shut up and came crying back to England.

Nargus is also claiming Feroz' mother-in-law was hitting him. How can she say that? She treats her own sons-in-law the same way.

Before the fight in June 1999, Ajmal packed all his things, including things he had given to his sons. He said to Fardeen, 'Why are you going to stay with your wife? You're about to get your stay in England, so pack your bags and come and live with me in Rochdale. Forget your wife'.

After Ajmal made his sons beat their wives and their father-in-law up, Ajmal went and sat in his daughter-in-law's brother's wife's relatives' house and told them it served his daughters-in-law right that his sons hit them. He swore at his daughters-in-law and their father, and told the relatives that his daughters-in-law were bad. They asked what gave him the right to say they were bad and for once Ajmal felt ashamed, and left.

Nargus phoned Ajmal's daughters-in-laws' relatives and told them to get the women to give her grandsons their stays in England and see a solicitor. She lied to the solicitor that Ajmal's daughters-in-laws' family had split her grandsons from their wives. The solicitor said he would have to talk to the daughters-in-law himself, so Nargus had to give him their phone number. When he phoned Feroz' wife and told her what Nargus had said, she was shocked and told the solicitor all that Nargus and her family had done. The solicitor said he would not take her case.

Ajmal thought he could use his daughters-in-law to call his sons to England, but they were wrong. Ajmal will not be able to use his daughters-in-law ever again.

Ajmal is saying he wants his sons to get back with their wives because shelves full of his dishes are still in their house. But that is not true. Before he went back to Pakistan all he had left in his daughters-in-laws' house were three glasses, three cups and two old pans, one with a broken handle and one without a lid.

Before Nagina went to Pakistan all she gave Fardeen and his wife for their new houses were secondhand spoons, knives and forks and a few used cups and a kettle, which they used themselves when they lived in their little house in Accrington. He took back the TV he gave them for their wedding. Ajmal could not even afford to feed his own daughter, and he had to borrow £3000 from the bank for his daughter's wedding. Yet he was still telling his daughters-in-laws' parents to provide a *daaj*. It was Ajmal and Nagina's responsibility to feed their daughters-in-law, not to dump their responsibilities on their parents.

People keep coming to Ajmal's house claiming he is a thief and owes them money. They are asking where he lives. His daughters-in-law gave his address in Pakistan.

Ajmal got Fardeen married off when he was only 16, and he left nothing for him when he went back to Pakistan. He was too busy thinking about the big house he was going to build in Pakistan and how he was going to compete with other rich people.

Nargus sends Feroz out all day so he doesn't make a mess in her house. Once he got measles and she did not want him in the house, so she kept trying to send him to other people's houses.

In Pakistan Ajmal's daughter would not talk to Feroz. She would call him her enemy. In England she ignored him and would not meet him, just because he liked his wife and not his Nan.

Nagina Ajmal told her daughters-in-law that her mother Nargus had tried to split her up from her husband. If this is true she should have stopped her.

Nagina's daughter told her sister-in-law her Nan was trying to teach her how to do *taveez* on people, but she must not tell her mother Nagina. She said 'Don't tell me things you haven't told your mother, I don't want to know'.

Ajmal sat in his daughters-in-laws' parents' house and said to their father, 'Who gives you the right to tell my sons off if they do something wrong? I'm their father, I will tell them myself. You should stay out of it.' The father replied, 'All right, from now I won't say a word to them'. 'Oh, so you want my sons to get bad habits then!' said Ajmal. Always he would twist people's words.

Once Ajmal invited Feroz and his wife to stay for a few days because he wanted to spend some time with his son. But instead of taking them to his house he took them straight to Nargus's house in Accrington. When Feroz' wife challenged this he said, 'What's it to you? You're going to stay where I tell you. Feroz will stay in his Nan's house and you will eat and sleep there too!'

Ajmal knew very well that Nargus would break up his son's marriage. But later Ajmal phoned Feroz' wife at Nargus' house and said, 'What are you doing there? I thought I told you to go to Rochdale.' 'But you dropped me off here yourself' said Feroz' wife. 'Oh so you're blaming me now!' said Ajmal. 'Don't answer me back. I will tell everyone that my daughter-in-law talks back to her father-in-law.'

When people hear about Ajmal's behaviour they say he must be psychotic. Everyone thinks he has something wrong in his head. Why did he build such a big house in Pakistan, when he can't afford to live in it or pay the bills to feed his family? It is because he wanted to compete with rich people and show them he could build a big house too. It was all for show. But Ajmal and his wife won't have any peace living there because it was built with money made from fraud. Ajmal has built a house of hell, and he will find no happiness there.

When Feroz' Nan was trying to trick another innocent girl into marrying her grandson for his stay in the UK, the girl found out and threw him out. That's when I sent this rhyme to Feroz' Nan:

Hey diddle diddle, hear this riddle
Everyone laughed to see such fun
When the dish ran away with the spoon.

The old woman with the long tongue and feet
Trotted from Norfolk Street to Richmond Street
Took a box of sweets and an engagement ring
And said she was the daughter of a king (Raja, a higher caste)
She pretended to be her grandson's mum
And took along the drunken bum
But the clever girl knew about the immigration case
And smacked the ring into his face.
The drunken bum said 'You gave your word'
The clever girl said 'Not after what I heard'
Get out you druggie, you drunk, you frauds
Or I'll call the police and claim the rewards
The old woman said, 'But you're my daughter!'
The clever girl stood her ground and fought her
Away ran the fraudsters without a trace
What a terrible, dreadful disgrace.

Just another chapter for our file
Another little thing that makes us smile.

CHAPTER EIGHT

Ajmal Rafiq and his wife have accused their daughter-in-law's family of so many bad things which are not true.

As for Nargus, she has no one in England. None of her relatives are talking to her and she does not get on with her sons-in-law. Yet still she will not give up destroying people's lives.

All Ajmal's daughters-in-law wanted to do was to live peacefully with their husbands, but Ajmal and Nargus would never let them do that. Splitting couples up is not just a trivial matter as she seems to think. But she has destroyed two couple's lives. God will show her the error of her ways and she will find no peace in life. What chance did Ajmal's daughters-in-law have of living with their husbands if their in-laws were against them like this?

Ajmal and his wife did not think about how hard it was for their married sons to settle into their homes. They should have supported them with good advice and helped them to live a good life.

Ajmal Rafiq's daughters-in-law thought their mother-in-law was OK until a few days before the fight, when she phoned their house and said to her son Feroz that he should try to get the £5000 from his wife and he only had to stay a month with his wife before going to his Nan in Accrington. She would take care of the rest.

Fardeen Rafiq's wife told her father-in-law that Fardeen was OK now and did not listen to his Nan Nargus. Ajmal Rafiq would get angry and say to his daughter-in-law, 'Is my son Fardeen all right? I will sort him out.' Ajmal took Fardeen out in his car and shouted at him for a whole hour, and when Fardeen came back into the house he did not want to know his wife any more.

Ajmal would say to his daughters-in-law in England, 'So what if my sons leave you? I'm not going to be in Pakistan to listen to people's gossip. All my family will come to England, and after that I don't care what anyone says about me or my family.' Now Ajmal Rafiq can hear what he has started.

If Nargus and Ajmal want to look for bad things in people then they should look at themselves, then they'll never run out of things to talk about.

Nargus's and Ajmal's families are each guilty of more sins than the whole of Ajmal's daughter-in-law's family. Someone should tell Ajmal and Nargus that they have now fallen into the grave they have dug for others. They should stop digging.

Ask Nagina why she hates her brothers-in-laws' wives. Nagina and Ajmal wind Shahid up and try to turn him against his wife. When Shahid bad-mouths his wife, they laugh at him. Then Ajmal goes round to people's houses and says 'I don't know why my brother and his wife don't get along, look at me and Nagina, we get along fine'. But Ajmal is the one responsible for turning his brother against his wife. After Ajmal causes a fight in his brother's house he tried to be good in front of people. Ajmal's daughters-in-law know this.

If Ajmal wanted a reconciliation he should have brought Nargus along with him, the one who winds him up. Instead Ajmal started making excuses not to come to the reconciliation, because his mother-in-law would not agree to come.

In Pakistan Nagina is blaming all sorts of people for splitting their sons up with their wives. If this was true then Ajmal's daughters-in-law would have said so, because they don't owe anyone anything.

Ajmal's daughters-in-law begged their father-in-law Ajmal not to split them up from their husbands, and Ajmal used to laugh in their faces. It was not a kind laugh but a wicked laugh. Now ask Ajmal who is begging and who is laughing. Somebody should tell his sons that their father has made a fool out of both of them because he has kept his own wife and split them up with theirs.

Later the family heard that Ajmal was asking his sons' *rishtay* from his daughter-in-laws' mother's nephew's house.

Before Ajmal asked for his daughter-in-laws' *rishtay* both he and his wife would be kind to their daughters-in-law. But as soon as they were married into the family, they became different people. They wanted to look for bad things in their daughters-in-law so that they could criticise them and split them up from their sons.

When Fardeen went to Accrington to meet his Uncle Shahid, who was going to Pakistan, he took all his wages with him. When he came back he told his wife he had given £10 to Kiran's child and £50 to Shahid for his family in Pakistan. But when Shahid was asked, he said he had never been given this money. He asked them to get Fardeen to the phone but he refused. Then Fardeen admitted that he had lied. He said he had bought a mobile phone with the money.

Ajmal's daughters-in-law felt sorry for him and said it was OK, but he would have to explain it to his father when he came to England. Fardeen said he would and his father would understand.

When Ajmal returned he said, 'I have been in Pakistan for nine weeks and I've been counting how much money my sons have earned. It comes to two thousand pounds, where is it?' They told him only Fardeen was working as Feroz was in Accrington, and there had been bills to pay. But when Ajmal asked his sons about it they both said they had given all their money to their wives. The women were shocked to hear these lies.

CHAPTER NINE

After Ajmal's sons beat their wives up, we prepared a case on them and went to our MP. We wanted to get both brothers sent back abroad. This is the correspondence.

House of Commons
9 November 1999
To: Immigration Office
Re: Taniya and Maaria

I have been approached by the above sisters about the problems regarding their estranged husbands, who are brothers. This case is rather complicated but I will make it as simple as possible.

Both my constituents tell me the family of their husbands in Pakistan planned that they should get married to gain entry to the UK and that the marriage was for this purpose. They indicated the poor and violent treatment they had received.

Their father-in-law, the father of the brothers, is, they claim, one of the root causes of the problem. His correct name is Ajmal Rafiq. He also uses a false name, which is the name he gave to the Immigration Service when he re-entered the country on a forged passport, having been thrown out originally as a failed asylum seeker a few years ago. They tell me his philosophy is never to pay any bills and to use fraud. This caused them considerable problems with household finances after they married their respective husbands. At one time, when Mr Rafiq was hiding from the police and others in my constituency, he hid a dozen or more of his spare credit cards, which they found only recently, and still have them in their possession.

My constituents are really upset at what has happened and feel as though their husband's family has exploited them.

I would be grateful for your confirmation that the authorities are doing everything possible to apprehend these two overstayers/illegals.

I look forward to hearing from you.
Jeff Rooker MP

To: Minister of State, Home Office
2 November 2000
Fardeen Rafiq, Feroz Rafiq and Ajmal Rafiq

Further to my recent letters of 18th and 30th October, I enclose yet another from my constituent. As you can see, the issue is getting to very serious proportions, which is the reason I am sending in a constant flow of material from my constituent. It is quite clear that these men are nasty characters.

From my files I do not appear to have received replies to my letters of 12th June (when I enclosed details of credit card misuse), 12th July and 29th October. The latest response I have is your letter of 25th August confirming that the information I sent in on 25th May had been added to the file.

We now have a situation of threats and potential use of firearms, which appears to require proactive work from the Home Office and police.

I look forward to hearing from you.

Nothing was done about this matter. The Home Office were just adding the information to the file and in the end did nothing. Both brothers are still in the UK.

HM Immigration Service
2 December 1999
Dear sir/madam
Re: AJMAL RAFIQ

Thank you for your recent letter concerning the above, who appears to be an immigration offender. You may be aware that we have recently dealt with his two sons, who we encountered in the Accrington area. We have not been able to apprehend Ajmal Rafiq and so any information concerning his whereabouts, place of work and any other addresses he uses would be of interest.
If you can provide any information on his whereabouts please write to me at the above address and I will seek to apprehend Mr Rafiq as quickly as possible.

Yours faithfully
Immigration Officer

Ajmal's daughters-in-law read in the Kitaab that the throne of the Shaytan (devil) Iblis is on the sea. He places his throne on the sea, then sends forth his armies. One of them comes and says he has done such and such and Iblis says he has done nothing. Another comes and says 'I did not leave him until I had split him from his wife'. He brings him closer and clasps him and says he did well. The Shaytan must be embracing Ajmal Rafiq and his mother-in-law Nargus, and telling them they did well.

THE END

Made in the USA
San Bernardino, CA
15 March 2014

TANWEER AKHTER